AGENT
FOR CHANGE

The Story of Pablo Steele
as told to
Gary MacEoin

ORBIS BOOKS ● MARYKNOLL, NEW YORK

*To Jim and Barbara, whose enduring friendship
and support carried me over many dark periods
and gave meaning to my life these past fifteen years,
with affection and gratitude.*

CONTENTS

FOREWORD

In the January 1971 issue of *The Lamp,* a Christian Unity magazine, an article appeared entitled, "Harvey Steele." Other articles in that issue included: "John XXIII," "Dorothy Day," "Dom Helder Camara," "Martin Luther King, Jr.," "Cesar Chavez," "Martin Buber," "Dietrich Bonhoeffer," "Mohandas Gandhi," and "Athenagoras I." The editors of *The Lamp* asked a group of professional writers to contribute to a special issue, the theme of which was: "The Fellowship of the Holy Spirit—People Who Count Today." Edward S. Skillin, editor of *Commonweal* magazine, chose to write on Harvey Steele. Here is a brief excerpt from that article.

At present he is devoting his considerable talents to the courses and demonstration projects of his Cooperative Institute in Panama City. Each term of several months brings together some 50 or 60 local leaders from a number of Latin American countries for ICI's intensive training in sound agronomy and cooperative techniques. These men then return home and organize their own people, even to the extent

of setting up their own training centers. Results are
thereby greatly multiplied.

The circles of his Christian service are widening.
Father Steele has helped 5,000,000 fellow-men, and
he hopes to help 5,000,000 more!

I have known Harvey Steele nearly twenty years. We
first met in the Dominican Republic at the home of a
mutual friend whom I was visiting. Padre Pablo, as he
was called, came to dinner one night; his hair was already
white, his calm, friendly face was deeply tanned. He
was wearing the customary white cassock and looked
more like a Hollywood extra than a missionary priest.
I had no idea I was meeting a tenacious social reformer.
He was too relaxed and too quiet to fit the image.

At the time I was twenty-seven, in my second year
at the major seminary and a veteran of two years of
military service. I thought I was an informed idealist,
but Harvey's thinking awakened me from my compla-
cency. I wanted to learn more about his work among
the poor. He agreed to take me on a tour of the villages
where he was training local leaders in the principles of
the cooperative movement. I knew next to nothing about
credit unions and consumer co-ops.

The next day we traveled bright and early, in old
clothes, over rough and muddy roads. For miles we did
not talk—the jarring and bouncing of the jeep made it
almost impossible. At the first village, and each one there-
after, we were greeted with wild enthusiasm by the black
natives. Signs of poverty were everywhere, but the people
looked happy. Their tiny shacks and lean bodies did not
seem to dishearten them. They washed themselves and
their clothing in the river; little boys went about naked
and women carried huge bundles on their heads. It was
a world very foreign to this American. I was amazed

at how gracefully Father Steele slipped into this culture. The men gathered around him like children around their instructor. Streams of unintelligible Spanish poured back and forth as they asked him questions and listened attentively to his replies, periodically bursting into gales of childish laughter. The women and children gathered on the perimeter of this circle to watch and listen. Harvey was in the middle generating a movement and excitement that I found irresistibly attractive. The same pattern was repeated in four different villages, each one giving us a wholehearted farewell as we left, with children and dogs racing beside our jeep.

I had seen missionaries among their people, but I had never seen this kind of spirit. It was an experience I shall never forget. I knew Father Steele had a special gift, but something deeper than personal talent was responsible for this trust and friendship between the priest and his people. He had obviously communicated his deep desire to help them to help themselves, and he had won their love and respect. In one day I was convinced of the power of the cooperative movement. This was not a cause, or a reform movement as such, it was a human process based on common sense, trust, friendship, and respect. I witnessed something quite rare that day: a foreigner, a white man, a priest at that, who was somehow the center of interest and concern for thousands of these back-village peasants. A Spanish-speaking Canadian, in the tropics, was teaching black Dominicans how to transform their poverty and despair into hope and prosperity.

These people had been living for years under the ruthless dictator Trujillo, and as meager as their produce was, he was stealing their land for his sugar crop. They were an exploited people and there were very few interested in helping them improve their lot. It was not very long after I returned to the States that I learned that Harvey's influence among the poor was soon viewed as a potential danger to the government. Trujillo was quick to move against any organized group because of their potential for resistance. Though Harvey had no interest in politics, his life was threatened and he was forced virtually at gunpoint to leave the Dominican Republic. Fifteen years of work had to be put aside. Fortunately, Trujillo could not destroy the Dominican co-op movement, which is still bearing good fruit today.

After my ordination to the priesthood, I learned more about the Cody Institute and the ideas of the co-op movement, and I tried in vain three times over the years to be released from my diocese to work with Father Steele. I was refused permission by two succeeding bishops. The Diocese of Paterson, New Jersey, had sent me to study for a Doctorate in Canon Law after ordination and they were not about to let me go off on some questionable crusade. In spite of this disappointment, over the years I have been able to help Father Steele in various ways to establish his new facilities in Panama. The extent of his success in the establishment of the Inter-American Cooperative Institute is one bright side of the Dominican disappointment. However, for a long time it has distressed me that the official Church has never really shown any interest in his work. A few individual chuchmen here and there were kind to him, and generous as well, but the idea of the Church working in the socioeconomic apostolate still has not come of age. Usually it has been the government people who have shown the most interest.

As the years move along, I see Harvey growing older, and I have been after him relentlessly for over five years to write his memoirs. Many other friends have urged the same thing. We feel strongly that this is a rare story, one which must be told, for the good of the Church of the future, as well as for the good of the community of man. After a struggle, Harvey finally agreed to do the book and we were fortunate to obtain the excellent services of Gary MacEoin to write the manuscript in collaboration with Harvey.

The finished work is now in your hands. It tells the story of one man's life in the service of his fellowman. It is a testimony of dedicated perseverance in the struggle for human dignity for all men. I am proud to have had a small part in bringing the book to life. I am proud to know the man: Harvey Steele.

Reverend John T. Catoir, J.C.D.
Officialis, Diocese of Paterson, N.J.

INTRODUCTION

A phone call from Father John Catoir started it. Would
I help Father Steele to write his life story? Father Catoir's
reasons for wanting to have that story placed on the record
are explained by him in the Foreword to this book. He
had won Father Steele's somewhat reluctant agreement.
But Father Steele, not being a professional writer, would
need to take a year off to do the job alone. His work
was too demanding, in too critical a stage of development,
and in his eyes too important for that. Hence the approach
to me. From their knowledge of my published work, both
on the socioeconomic problems of Latin American and
on the impact of Vatican Council II on the Catholic
Church's self-understanding, Father Steele and Father
Catoir thought I could quickly grasp what Father Steele
was trying to do and help him present it in a proper
perspective.

My response was guarded. Having been through this
experience more than once before, I knew some of the
pitfalls. The relationship created has some of the elements
of that of spiritual director to penitent and of psychoana-
lyst to patient. It is necessary to dig deep. What a man

does is not nearly so important as why he does it. In addition, it is all-important that the collaborator share the enthusiasms and ambitions of the principal. Otherwise, the collaborator may report fairly, but it is hardly possible for him to project the spirit without distortion.

I had, of course, heard of Father Steele and his work as a pioneer in the cooperative movement in Latin America. But my information was mostly at second hand. I had no way of knowing how faithfully it reflected the reality. We agreed that I should go and see for myself, with no commitment on either side.

I moved into the Inter-American Cooperative Institute in Panama while a course for some thirty students from all over Latin America was in progress. I met the students individually and in class situations. I read the manuscript of a textbook Father Steele had written as a synthesis and summary of what he wanted to get across to them. I talked with him far into the night, since he was usually too busy to talk much during the day. I read everything available he had written or that others had written about him.

What I saw and heard I liked. The Institute was undoubtedly doing a good job. But I wanted one further proof. How much of what the students learned survived the transfer from classroom to the life situation? The nearest place to get a real view of what graduates of the Institute were doing in the field was Veraguas in western Panama. The trip involved more than twelve hours by jeep in tropical heat, much over rough roads, but it was worth it. I met half a dozen young men and women, most of them several years out of the Institute, none of them in any way dependent on Father Steele. Some worked for cooperatives, others for community projects of government departments. They knew their business. They were good technicians. But in addition, and this is unfortunately rare in Latin America, they were dedicated young people, fired with a determination to make their lives count, to contribute to the betterment of their own people. They were true missionaries. Father Steele had marked them for ever.

That experience decided me. I had found a man I could myself believe in, and I could feel proud for the rest of my life if I succeeded in helping others to understand what he stood and worked for, and why he stood and worked for it.

Father Steele projects himself principally as a man of action. He does not work out an elaborate theoretical analysis and evaluation of a situation as a first step. Rather he decides, almost instinctively, that the conventional solutions are getting nowhere, then applies his own. What is impressive is the prophetic quality of his instinct.

In China, as a young man, he saw the ineffectiveness of an approach to the missions which had gone unchallenged for generations. Not until the Second Vatican Council, nearly a quarter of a century later, did any significant sector of Catholic pastoral and theological thought catch up with him.

In Latin America his instinctive grasp of realities long hidden from most of those around him similarly forced him reluctantly into unpopular roles of prophecy and witness. Today, a significant and growing number of missionaries share his rejection of activities which in fact fostered superstition and supported the oppressor in his dehumanization of the poor. They agree that to be a Christian one must first be human, and that it is not possible to be human while living in subhuman conditions.

A significant and growing number of concerned Latin Americans and their friends have similarly come to agree with him that the development programs sponsored by the rich countries and their oligarchic allies in Latin

American governments are incapable of helping the people, that salvation must ultimately come from the people themselves.

Father Steele avoids the temptation of seeing his particular program, the cooperative movement, as a universal cure-all. I was particularly impressed by his account of the failure of his first efforts in the Dominican Republic, a failure he attributes to the quality of the human material he was working with. I do not know of any scientific attempt to establish the line of moral and cultural deprivation below which the cooperative approach is inoperable. The success of Father Steele's initiatives in other parts of the Dominican Republic and in other countries would suggest that most of Latin America is above that line. Today, nevertheless, we are forced to recognize the uncomfortable fact that the highest population growth is in the lowest stratum of Latin American society, and that the living conditions for the poor in the hemisphere are deteriorating, not improving. The issue is, in consequence, far from academic.

Equally realistic is Father Steele's evaluation of the limits to the impact which the cooperative movement can exercise in a society in which all power is concentrated in the hands of the few. He agrees with his famous mentor, Dr. Moses Coady, who developed the Antigonish method of cooperativism. "We have to get over the naive idea," Coady once said, "that monopolistic exploiters and dictators are going to reform because good men preaching justice and charity tell them to do so. Experience has shown that bad men generally will reform only when they have to. We must, therefore, add force to our persuasion. This does not mean physical force and bloodshed, but it does call for the force of ideas expressed in terms of a program that will give a legitimate share of power to the people."

Time and again, Father Steele has seen a cooperative

movement grow in a region to the point where it was acquiring a share of power, threatening the arbitrary control of landlords and moneylenders only to be snuffed out or reduced to impotence by the violent power of those who manipulated the armed might of the state. He saw it in the Dominican Republic. At first, Trujillo favored a movement he hoped to use. When he realized his mistake, he crushed it. A similar fate befell the Galán experiment started in the mid-1960's in the slums of Bogotá by Marymount nuns from the United States, helped by Camilo Torres and other Colombian priests and nuns. The state authorities quickly recognized the threat to the oligarchic system, expelled the United States nuns, jailed several of the Colombian priests, and persuaded the church authorities to cooperate in silencing the priests and nuns as subversives. That action convinced Camilo Torres that no progress could be made by working within the structures and drove him to join the guerrillas.

So it goes throughout Latin America. There is not yet any situation in which it is possible to say with certainty that the vicious circle has been broken. I recently had the opportunity to discuss this key issue with Paulo Freire, the Brazilian educator who has been in exile since a military dictatorship took over his homeland in 1964 and who is now director of education for the World Council of Churches in Geneva. The Freire method, which teaches literacy to peasants while simultaneously developing in them an understanding of the factors which keep them in poverty and a commitment to struggle together to break the cycle, has been outlawed in Brazil but is used widely by missionaries and other progressive teachers throughout Latin America.

Dr. Freire, whose outlook closely parallels that of Father Steele, also shares his experience in this respect. He can point to places in all parts of the world in which the poor have been aroused and committed themselves to take the first steps toward liberation. But quickly, the forces of reaction have rallied and have either stamped out the movements or domesticated them.

He believes, nevertheless, that there has been progress and that one of these days it will expand and coalesce so as to become irreversible. A similar faith drives Father Steele to continue. He is encouraged particularly by the development of the theology of liberation among Latin American Christians, by the growing number of priests and Protestant clergymen, and also of nuns and other teachers, both from Latin America and from abroad, who regard themselves as involved in a historic process of freeing mankind from material and spiritual bondage. He is heartened when he sees them turn to the cooperative method as an effective tool to promote this process. I for my part am sure that his life story and experience will encourage many more to commit themselves to the task of freeing men in all their dimensions, and that makes me proud to have helped in the creation of this book.

Gary MacEoin

1

NOVA SCOTIA

Heritage of the Scottish Highlands

As far back as I can remember, I understood the need for cooperation, especially if you are poor and at the mercy of people for whom money counts more than justice. When I was a boy of eleven, I was in the crowd as we burned the local company store and looted it. Those were bad years for the workers and their families in the mining areas of Nova Scotia, because of the depression that followed the First World War, the Great War as we used to call it, in the belief that men could never again stage carnage and destruction to match it. In 1922 alone, the town of Dominion was idle for nine months, as was the entire surrounding area.

The mines were owned by foreign interests, from England and the United States, to whom the provincial authorities had sold Nova Scotia's most important assets many years earlier, and with whom these same authorities still continued in collusion to block the efforts of the United Mine Workers to secure a living wage and establish human conditions of work. All we had to keep us

alive during the strikes was the dole. I can remember
as clearly as if it were yesterday how the miners would
come down the street every Friday afternoon, each man
carrying a little white bag like a pillowslip. That little
bag held the family rations for the coming week, some
flour, some corn meal, some lard, a scrap of meat or
fish, butter, sugar, and salt.

It was in those circumstances that idleness and frustration led the people to violence. Everything in the town,
above ground as well as below, was owned by the company. The priests used to warn us that it was a sin to
damage company property, and that we would have to
make restitution before they would absolve us. But we
paid no heed. We did what we had to do. We knew
instinctively, as many years later I learned when I read
St. Thomas Aquinas, that a man has a right to take from
the surplus wealth of the rich what he needs to maintain
his family and himself.

Soon, also, we learned another lesson. It is not enough
to have right on your side if you lack power. Twice they
declared martial law and brought the militia in from
Ottawa to drive us off the streets and hold us under
curfew from eight in the evening. And the broken men
had finally to crawl back on the employer's conditions,
heartened only by their determination to recoup their
strength and then make another try in more favorable
circumstances. But about one thing we were clear. We
knew who were our friends and who our enemies. In
later life, whether in China or in Latin America, when
I saw the exploitation of the poor and weak by the rich
and powerful, when I saw law and authority prostituted
to maintain injustice, I needed no "outside agitator" to
convince me that the analysis of the capitalist system
made by Karl Marx has to be taken seriously.

In later life, I have inevitably added to my store of
knowledge and understanding, learning many things by

trial and error, changing emphases and developing new techniques as I go through life. Yet even today I can see quite clearly the basic stamp put on my character by my youthful experience. It was in my native Nova Scotia that I confronted the reality and recognized the wickedness of exploitation of the poor by the rich and powerful. There also I learned what the poor must do in order to get out of the trap. They have to cultivate personal habits of hard work and thrift, and then they have to join together, pooling their efforts and their tiny savings until they constitute a counterforce able to humble the proud and infuse terror into the heart of the exploiter. During that long wait, no sign of the vengeance in their heart must show on their inscrutable face, even when with hat in hand they surrender their sons to be killed and their daughters to be violated.

Neil MacNeil, who subsequently acquired considerable fame as a newsman and author in the United States, grew up in Nova Scotia some twenty years before I did. He was in fact my third cousin. Neil some years ago described his boyhood experiences in a book *The Highland Heart in Nova Scotia* which made all the neighbors mad, but which nevertheless captured some of the essence of that very special community. And the type of life and people he described had changed little between his time and mine.

The traditions, he said, are the traditions of the Scots, a mixture of pride and simplicity, of pugnacity and kindness. Most of the people had come from the Highlands of Scotland or the island chain of the Hebrides just to the west of northern Scotland, and they were Gaelic-speaking Roman Catholics. The Gaelic, as Neil noted, was a great tongue for cussing and praying. They were sure of themselves, those people. They took greatness for granted, and they knew no superiors in their own minds. They tilled the unproductive farms with a maximum of physical effort and a minimum of machinery. They fished in the lakes, hunted and cut wood in the forests. The work was in large part seasonal, with long intervals of rest, especially in the winter when the snow enveloped everything, swamping the trees, filling the hollows, banked up to the eaves of the houses. The men drank Jamaica rum, tossing it back in a single gulp. They smoked black, strong plug tobacco, in black, strong pipes. They like to talk and sing and fight. Nobody ever locked a door, and you could walk into any neighbor's home without knocking. Burglary, robbery, crimes of sex and violence, all were absolutely unknown.

On such a farm and among such people I formed my first impressions of the world. I was born in Sydney, Nova Scotia, then a small city of about 25,000 people, on May 3, 1911, but I moved to my grandparents' farm near Beechmont in 1914 and there I spent the following seven years. My father was a steel worker in Sydney and was away from home most of the time, so that I was deeply under the influence of my grandfather who worked the farm. When I was five, I had a burst appendix which nearly killed me, and the recuperation was slow. But that did not mean any kind of soft regime. We were poor people, and during those years of the First World War, food was never in abundance. Canada did indeed produce more than enough food to satisfy the needs of all Canadians, but at that time English interests still controlled the economy, and food was exported to England while many of us were on tight rations. As the eldest child in a family that grew steadily to the number of fourteen (of whom ten still live), I had quickly to share responsibility with my mother. I completed the first five grades of school in a little red schoolhouse which expressed the same frugality as the rest of our lives. There were no paper or pencils for our exercises. Instead, we added, substracted, multiplied, and divided on the old-style slate, rubbing it clean before storing it away for the next time. The stress in those schools was on memory, and we spent long hours practicing our multiplication tables and learning poems and aphorisms from the well-thumbed Reader.

Our diet was often meager. The bread was of poor quality, baked from flour that had perhaps been salvaged from a sunken ship. And our clothing in winter was seldom adequate for the weather. Cold hands and feet were normal, and we looked forward to the spring when the green grass would reappear, the first flowers would peep from the long-frozen ground, and the birds would build their nests and lay their eggs. But I had little time to search for nests, or to hunt fox, otter, rabbits, or partridge. After school, and at weekends and vacation time, there were endless chores in the house and outside, milking cows, tending crops, sawing firewood.

My father had worked from the time when he was fourteen years old, in the Sydney steel plant. But work was scarce and in 1921 he decided to try coal mining. He found himself a job in Dominion, a town of three or four thousand people near the bigger town of Glace Bay. Both towns had grown up around coal mines, and the company ran everything, the land, the houses, the stores. It was just like Wales, a perfect replica of the way of life presented in *How Green Was My Valley,* the same hunger, the same tragedy, the same impotence. The fear hung like a pall all day, every day, from the time the worker left until you heard him lift the latch as he returned. I never did work in the mines, but I lived that daily eternity. And later, as a young priest, I saw it many times, when called to administer the last rites to men who were trapped in a cave-in. The shafts were sunk near the shore and then went out five to ten miles under the ocean. You could smell the salt water which was always dripping, no matter how strongly they propped up the overhead with pit timbers. I remember the first time, when I was taken out ten miles under the sea in an electric train to anoint an Italian man crushed by falling stone. That was the usual thing, the most common kind of accident, the collapse of an inadequately supported roof when they were blasting out the coal. Sometimes it was gas, sometimes an explosion. But always it was terror.

When we came to the town of Dominion in 1921, the company had stopped building any more houses for workers, and the only place we could get was a few rooms downstairs in the Salvation Army headquarters. It brought us right into the middle of the activity, because the United Mine Workers hall was upstairs in the same building. But that didn't mean that I could just hang around all day. I was still going to school. In addition, in view of the many strikes and the acute shortage of everything, my mother and I quickly began to develop supplementary income sources. So I built up a newspaper route and she parlayed a number of odds and ends into a cow. And by 1923 or thereabouts, we were ready for our big move, a double move. Pooling our capital of about $250, we rented a house to which we could transfer from the Salvation Army building and also start a small business selling candy, newspapers, and things of that sort. Actually, my father never went back to the mines after this. We all pitched in together and made a great success of the store, which within four or five years expanded to become the biggest business in town. My parents are of contrasting temperaments. My mother is the essential Scot, dour, puritanically rigid, hard-working, serious, long-suffering, totally honest, and deeply serious. My father would pass anywhere for an Irishman, a great humanist, kind, outgoing, generous, always ready for a prank. Indeed, although the Steeles came to the New World from Scotland nearly two hundred years ago, he claimed an Irish background, and he always lived up to it. These two contrasting temperaments, each in its own way, contributed to the success of the store, my father by his way with customers, my mother by her concern for every detail of the business. The amount of work grew ferociously as the store expanded. Before long, I was so crushed under it that I dropped out of high school without completing the third year and reconciled myself to spending the rest of my life behind a counter in a moribund mining town. Or at least I thought I had no alternative. But a couple of my friends didn't agree. One was a cousin named Joe MacDonald. He was some years older than I and at this time he had been several years in the university. He came to visit us while home on vacation, and he argued very forcefully both with my parents and with me that I should go back to school. At that time my uncle Rod was Grand Knight of the Knights of Columbus in Sydney, and he said I should apply for a scholarship offered by the Knights. I took the examinations, only to read in due course in the newspaper that another applicant had won. Uncle Rod, however, was not satisfied. He wanted to know just how well I had done, and as Grand Knight of a Chapter he was able to carry his inquiry to the source. To his surprise and chagrin, he discovered that I had been cheated out of the scholarship. I had scored an aggregate of 894 points in the examination. The "winner," whose family had some influence, had scored only 791. Uncle Rod raised such a ruckus that the priest in charge agreed to give two scholarships, and I was on my way to the academy or high school associated with St. Francis Xavier University in Antigonish.

Away from home for the first time, I enjoyed myself. I started boxing, managed the hockey team, played football and basketball, and was alumni editor of the university magazine. Naturally, my marks suffered, and naturally I received a notice that if I didn't improve, the scholarship—which was for four years—would not be renewed after the first year. I didn't want that, so I began to study seriously and quickly jumped from a passing average right up to 85 or 90 percent. I went home for vacation feeling rather pleased with myself, only to get a letter notifying me that the scholarship had been canceled. The letter gave two reasons, first, that my marks were too low, and secondly, that I was obviously not planning to become a priest since I was taking science. I was furious. I had lifted my marks way up after I got the warning. There had been no condition in the scholarship that restricted it to potential seminarians, and even if there had been, I was doing a double major, classics as well as science. But I had no redress. My uncle was no longer Grand Knight, so he had lost his clout. The other recipient, who happened to be and has always remained my friend, retained his scholarship, but ironically he never did become a priest. As for me, I must have been too proud to give in. I took what I had saved on my newspaper route, with whatever supplement my mother could add, and I went back the next year. From that time I took a salary each summer for working in the store, and so I went on from one year to the next.

The scholarship incident, nevertheless, left a lasting scar. What I could see was the phoniness and the dishonesty of the priest and of his cronies who could manipulate behind the scenes and were above challenge. It made me question, probably for the first time, the whole validity of the claims of religion. Up to that time, religion had never been a major factor in my life, but neither had it been an issue. It was just something that was there and was taken for granted. My parents and grandparents were Catholic, enjoying the deep old-fashioned faith that was a pride and a tradition, a faith with a substantial admixture of Jansenism, as was then common, and also with its share of Celtic superstitions. While we lived in the country with my grandparents, we went to Mass in a mission chapel of the parish of Boisdale. It was a two hour drive by horse and buggy, and in summer we went once or twice a month. During the five winter months we were snowed in most of the time, and in consequence we rarely got to church. People received the sacraments a couple of times a year. I had never gone to a Catholic school, and I had very little formal instruction in my religion. The only priest I could say I ever knew up to then was Father Michael Gillis. He had grown up on a farm adjoining that of my mother's family, and when he was assigned to his first parish about 1918 or 1919, after he came back from war service as a chaplain, it was near my grandparents' home, and he would occasionally drop in when he happened to be passing.

It was only when I went to Antigonish in 1927 that I came for the first time into close continuing association with priests and with young men preparing for the priesthood. By this time I had rather firmly decided to pursue a professional career in which I could do something to improve the conditions of poor people like those with whom I had grown up. It was also clear that the practical alternatives were medicine and the Church; but my ambivalence was such that I continued to pursue courses that would permit me to choose one or the other. So I completed the premedical course and had also reached a point where I lacked just two subjects from the bachelor's degree that would qualify me to enter the seminary for theological studies. But following the scholarship incident I had grown more and more rebellious and discontented. I stopped going to church and started to drink beer and wine. One of the priests who taught us, a Father Nicholson, had decided I should be a priest, and he bombarded me with invitations to join his church choir and other activities. He meant well, but his psychology was terrible. So one day I made up my mind. I walked out without completing my bachelor's degree and went off to Toronto to enroll in medical school. The die, I thought, was cast.

Toronto was a whole new world. Up to that time, I had traveled little beyond the immediate vicinity of my parents' home and that of my grandparents. Even when I had gone to Antigonish to study, it was to a boarding school supervised by priests and run almost as strictly as a seminary. Here I was on my own, one of fifteen thousand students in what was reputed at that time to be the largest educational center in the British Empire. There were many others like myself, so it didn't take long to find a few friends who became my companions. For a while I thought I was having a great time, studying enough to get by. But the euphoria didn't last. I didn't find the medical studies as absorbing as I had hoped. I couldn't rid from my mind the lurking suspicion that I was running away from my first choice, the priesthood, and that medicine was only a substitute.

So I would start to think that perhaps I should go back to Antigonish, but what would immediately come to my mind would be the priest who had cheated me out of the scholarship, or Father Nicholson and his choir, or maybe some of the things I had seen and the stories I had heard of the priests siding with the bosses against the poor. There was the time in 1909 that people were always talking about, just two years before I was born. The parish priest, they said, had permitted the militia to place guns on the church steps during a strike. There were old men around, Irish and Scots, who had never again attended church. And I could remember myself that the pastor had a heated stable for his horse in the winter when the only heating we had was a stove in the kitchen. Among all those poor people he was reputedly the richest priest in all Canada. He didn't even have to ask us for money. It was an arrangement with the mine owners, an automatic check-off from every miner's wages, the same as the check-off for the grocery bill in the company store. There it was on my father's envelope when he came home Friday evening, 40 cents for the church. That wasn't my church. I couldn't see myself hobnobbing with the judge, the medical doctor, and the mine manager, honking the horn of a big automobile to clear the way as I hurried off for a round of golf.

The Call of the Seminary

When I thought I had everything straightened out, I would ride out to a small town called Scarboro, which is today a suburb of Toronto, to visit Jim McGilvray, a friend who had joined a group of foreign missionaries popularly known as the Scarboro Fathers. Jim was due to leave soon for China, then the one mission of the Scarboro Fathers, and by chance China was fairly prominent in the news. That was the year of the Japanese occupation of Manchuria and the creation of the puppet state of Manchukuo. The Japanese had also seized part of northern China and attacked Shanghai. It was the first phase of the Sino-Japanese War, which would continue intermittently for more than a decade and finally become merged into World War II. What my friend told me about poverty, sickness, and oppression in China made it clear to me that they needed both doctors and priests over there. I began to consider the possibility of joining him as a doctor, but when I saw what he was planning to do as a priest, I would also ask myself if there wasn't something to be said for the priesthood. And I had to admit that even back home there were priests like my mother's friend, Father Mike Gillis, the pastor in Boisdale, a humble man, loved and trusted by everyone because of his honesty. There was no doubt about his sympathy for the underdog. And although I didn't then know the details, I knew he had been one of the founders of the Extension Department of St. Francis Xavier University which had started in 1928. When I was in high school and at college in Antigonish, he used to visit there every summer from his parish, and he always looked me up. The idea of the Extension Department was to bring the university to the people, to go out on the weekends and talk to fishermen, farmers, and miners, telling them about social justice and the call for a just order contained in the papal encyclicals, urging them not to rely on coal but to join together and form credit unions and make themselves independent. That was the kind of priest I could identify with.

So there I was, still rebellious, still trying to sort out all the conflicting ideas, when I came home for the summer to work in the family store and make money for the following year of medical school. During the summer I drove up to Antigonish for the ordination to the priesthood of six seminarians. I had been friendly with two of them while I was in college at Antigonish, although they were three or four years older than me. One was my cousin, Joe MacDonald. The other, Mickey MacDonald (no relation), was a good friend, and our friendship has survived the years and the distance. He lived his entire life in rural and mining-town parishes in Nova Scotia, always studying and reflecting in the solitude of the long winters. Today he is blind, but his mind remains keen and committed. My friend from Scarboro, Jim McGilvray, was also present. It was a big occasion, and it made a deep impression on me. I had never seen an ordination ceremony before, and afterwards I couldn't put it out of my mind. I thought about it all the way back home. I thought about it all that night and the next one and the one after that. It was really getting me down, so that my mother saw there was something wrong and wanted to call the doctor. But all that was wrong was that I was fighting inside myself. About a week later, Joe MacDonald, the cousin who had been ordained, stopped by to greet my parents and give them his first blessing as a priest. My mother must have said something to him, because he took me aside and gave me a real pep talk. "I know you're not sure," he said, "but there is only one way to find out. I know Dr. Nicholson rubbed you the wrong way by trying to rush you, but that shouldn't be the deciding factor. You have to make up your mind for yourself."

I knew Joe was right. I had to stop running. So I wrote to the Scarboro Fathers, or to give them their official title, the Scarboro Foreign Mission Society of Canada, and they accepted me into what was then called the China Mission Seminary. The Society was not a religious order in the traditional sense. It was an association of secular or diocesan priests who accepted the leadership of the superior general in much the same way as priests in an ordinary diocese acccept that of their bishop, and who are assigned by him to work in whatever foreign missions Rome allots to this particular society. It had been founded about the time of the First World War by a Canadian priest, John Mary Fraser. Father Fraser was one of the great missionaries of the first half of this century, and he anticipated the mission philosophy of the Second Vatican Council in his insistence that established dioceses in the developed countries should share part of their abundance of priests with the growing churches of the mission territories. He in fact played a part in the founding of four of the twelve or fifteen major modern mission organizations, the Maryknoll Fathers in the United States, the Columban Fathers in Ireland, a similar society in Spain, and the Scarboro Fathers in English-speaking Canada.

I was given credit for the two years of philosophy

I had completed in college, leaving me with one more year of philosophy and four of theology. I was ordained to the priesthood in 1936, at the end of my third year of theology.

The seminary was for me a mixed experience. It started off well, for I was buoyed up by the experience known as first fervor. The spartan regime, up at 5:30 every morning, long hours of prayer, study, and silence, meals at fixed hours, lights out at 9:45 in the evening, all that was child's play as far as I was concerned. I was really convinced that I was on the right road, that I had found my vocation; and that is a conviction that has survived all the vicissitudes of the subsequent years. But otherwise, my life was far from pleasant. There were eleven of us in the class, and I was a few years older than most of them. In addition, I was a true son of my mother as far as my outlook on life was concerned, hard-working, serious, puritanically rigid. I took the rule much more seriously than some of the others. I remember we were just a few months in the seminary when the rector gave a lecture on what he called "particular friendships." It seemed that the seminarian could have no special friends. He had to behave the same to everyone. It was a rule, and to break it meant all kinds of dreadful, if unspecified, dangers. I was completely at a loss. All my years in college and in medical school I had circulated with my own group of friends, and I never saw any wrong in it. In addition, I already had lined up a couple of friends in the seminary. That night after supper, one of them came up and suggested we go for a walk. "What do you mean?" I said. "You heard the rector, didn't you? It's against the rules." "Who pays attention to rules?" he said. "That's a lot of nonsense." I thought it was nonsense myself, but it was the rule, so I broke with him. And I also broke with the other man.

They were angry and it was not long until one of them

got me in trouble with the rector. What happened was this. I was discussing the coal mines and the way the workers were exploited, and defending John L. Lewis. "You're a Communist," somebody challenged me. And indeed most of them saw nothing wrong with the silence of the Church in the face of injustice and with the benefits the priests received from the exploiters in return for their silence. So the story went around from one mouth to another, and soon I was on the carpet in the rector's room. "Is it true," he asked, "that you believe in labor unions, that you approve of what John L. Lewis is doing, that you were yourself involved in burning down company stores?" I admitted that all that was true. "Those are no ideas for a priest," he said. "If you want to stay here, you'll have to change your outlook. You can't keep on disseminating such ideas and infecting innocent people."

So I learned to keep my mouth shut and keep my thoughts to myself. I didn't blame the rector personally, because I knew he was saying what he had been taught and what he believed. But I was shocked to find myself in a system that forbade you to think for yourself, that tried to dictate your judgment on evident facts. And I was doubly hurt to see that they made a big fuss about a man who lived up to what he believed, while others could violate rules with impunity. Apparently you could do whatever you liked so long as you didn't challenge the system. So I went through the rest of the seminary in tension with the rector, in tension with my companions, in tension with myself. If this is what I have to do to get to China, this is what I'm going to do, I told myself; and this is what I did.

But getting to China wasn't going to be that easy. In 1932, Japan left the League of Nations rather than accept its ruling that the occupation of Manchuria was illegal. In the following years it continued to bite off further

chunks of northern China, and in 1936 and 1937 the incidents escalated into full-scale war. Peking and Tientsin
were taken and a protracted battle for Shanghai began.
A coastal blockade put an end to international travel,
isolating the Scarboro mission in central China for what
might prove to be years.

In the circumstances, all I could do was to return to
my native diocese of Antigonish for temporary assignment. When the pastor of Dominion, where I had grown
up and where my family still lived, heard of it, he asked
the bishop to assign me to Dominion as assistant. It was
the last thing I wanted, going back as a priest where
for years I had run a store. But he insisted, and I am
glad he did, because I learned a terrific amount that year.
The first thing I did was to visit every house in the parish.
The pastor tried to dissuade me. "We had the parish
census last year," he said. But I continued my rounds
because I knew the alternative was to move into the
bridge circle, become a member of the Establishment.
We had 850 families stretched out in an oval that was
seven or eight miles from one end to the other. By the
time I finished, we had to start an extra Mass on Sunday
because an extra thousand people were coming.

By that time also, I had become more acutely aware
than ever of the enormous need for decent housing, and
I had discovered how to do something about it. In a
word, I had become actively involved in the cooperative
movement.

The pastor in an adjoining parish, a man about thirty
years my senior, was the one who was responsible for
the breakthrough in housing. It was the custom in that
part of Canada to address a priest who had done graduate
work and earned the degree as Doctor rather than Father,
and this priest was known as Dr. Jimmy Tompkins, just
as the man with whom he had long been associated in
the development of the Extension Department of St.

Francis Xavier University, Antigonish, was known and
continues to be known in history as Dr. Moses Coady.
It was Father Tompkins who in 1921 started the People's
School that expanded in 1928 into the Extension Department under Father Coady. I had known them both when
I was in college, though across the chasm which at that
time separated the professor from the student. Jimmy
was a small man with a high-pitched voice. He weighed
about 110 pounds. But he had a mind that was going
all the time. He wasn't a good public speaker, preferring
to buttonhole people and get his point across to one person
at a time. Coady, who was some fifteen years younger,
was a total contrast. A big man who could have doubled
for Jack Dempsey, he had a perfect public manner. A
friend once said that he looked as if Rodin had hewn
him, with a blunt chisel, out of granite rock. They were
double first cousins, both from the Margaree Valley on
Cape Breton, of Irish stock. Their parents were modestly
successful farmers who were locally known as "drivers,"
that is, hard workers, dawn-to-dusk toilers in the mixed
type of farming common in eastern Nova Scotia.

Tompkins studied theology in Rome, as Coady did
subsequently. When he returned, he was named vice-
rector of St. Francis Xavier University, which was then
a very small school. His ideas were already radical for
the time. He wanted, for example, to amalgamate all
the fifteen or twenty universities in the Maritime Provinces, Catholic and Protestant. His other concern was
with social justice. All around him he saw hunger. The
city of Sydney had grown to 40,000 people, all dependent
on a steel mill which at that time was the biggest in the
British Empire. It brought the ore from Newfoundland
and the coal was all around. But the steelworkers and
the coal workers, as well as their families, were poor
and powerless, and so were the farmers and the fishermen. Searching for a solution, Father Tompkins went

back to Europe, and there he studied the cooperative movement in England and in Scandinavia. The information he brought back with him provided the starting point for the Antigonish movement. His first associates in starting the People's School were Father Hugh McPherson, a priest with degrees in agronomy and biology, Father Coady, an educationist, Father Boyle, whose degree was in philosophy, and Father Mike Gillis. All the pioneers were priests. The government would do nothing, and the people lacked the power and the knowledge to take the first step. With the Extension Department in 1929 they brought in some laymen, including A. B. MacDonald and Alex MacIntyre. They started going out on weekends to talk to the fishermen, farmers, and miners, just talking about social justice at first, the papal encyclicals and so on, then after a while encouraging the workers to start credit unions.

Actually the credit union movement was not new in Canada. Alfonse Desjardins, a French Canadian newspaperman who had studied in Europe, brought back the idea of the Raiffeisen credit union at the turn of the century, starting the first such union in the New World at Levis, Quebec, in 1900. Two years later, he founded the first credit union in the United States in New Hampshire, a state with many French-speaking inhabitants originally from Quebec. Both these unions were established in Catholic parishes. Before his death, Desjardins had founded more than 200 such groups in his native Quebec, most of them in Catholic parishes. Desjardins, however, had practically no impact in English-speaking Canada. But his movement was taken up in the United States by Edward Albert Filene of Boston, a Jewish philanthropist who spent more than a million dollars of his personal fortune promoting legislation and spreading the credit union idea. In 1931, Father Tompkins asked Roy Bergengren, an assistant to Filene, to come to Nova Scotia and to show them how to run credit unions successfully. Other kinds of cooperatives, production and consumer, followed quickly. By the middle of the 1930's, the fame of Antigonish was established. When the Wall Street crash of 1929 was followed by the Great Depression, people began to look for a new solution to their economic woes. *Collier's* and *The Saturday Evening Post* were telling their readers about the miracles happening in Nova Scotia. With bread lines a mile long in Detroit, Walter Reuther and other labor leaders were becoming interested. Motorcades of hundreds of automobiles were driving up from the United States to see for themselves.

That was the situation when I was assigned to Dominion after I finished my theology studies, and Father Tompkins was making history in the next parish. He had found an old law on the books of the Province, going back many years, under which the government advanced nearly the entire cash outlay for cooperative housing. Apparently it had never been used. Jimmy, however, found that it was for real, and he started off with a group of about twenty miners to put up the first cooperative village in North America. The situation in my parish was just the same as in his, houses fifty to eighty years old, in hopeless disrepair, and an acute shortage even of such dilapidated housing. He was delighted when I expressed an interest, because he had failed to strike a spark among any of the younger neighboring priests. I went up there every morning for three months to get a full understanding of what was involved, then started work with a group of my own. I was in a hurry, because I didn't know when I might be notified that a ship for China was available. So I assumed responsibility for much more than I would today. I dashed around, hiring carpenters, negotiating land purchase, ordering materials. But it worked out. The project was sufficiently advanced and the cooperative members sufficiently instructed, before I left, to be able to carry on from there on their own.

For the people of Dominion it was a significant step toward a better life. And for me personally it was a great boon and a great grace. I had proof direct of the correctness of Father Coady's assertion that the cooperative method is a blueprint for progress, that it is the road to power for the people. I accepted fully Father Tompkins' commission as I was about to set out for my mission. "I wish to God I was young like you," he said, "and had this opportunity to bring these teachings of justice to the millions of poor in China. And whatever you do, don't forget to get a credit union started as soon as you can."

War conditions all the time I was in China prevented a literal execution of the assignment. But even there I fulfilled the spirit of the mandate, and later I was able to demonstrate that my training was not wasted.

2

CHINA

First Glimpse of the Country at War

The Sino-Japanese War entered a new phase in 1938 with the completion of the occupation of Shanghai by the Japanese. By then they were in secure possession not only of Peking and Tientsin but of Nanking, the national capital. And they had deployed their armies to gain control of Soochow, Amoy, Hankow, and Canton, all of which would be theirs by the end of that year. With the Chinese driven back to a temporary capital at Chungking far in the interior, the Japanese were steadily extending their grip over the major cities, the roads, and the railroads, thus gaining a network of control. But even in the eastern coastal area over which they had swept, guerrilla fighting continued, and the countryside and smaller towns remained in Chinese hands.

During all these titanic struggles and convulsions, the Japanese were anxious to persuade world opinion that they were involved in nothing more than a "local police action." No sooner had they secured a firm hold on Shanghai, accordingly, than they reopened the port to international shipping. And so, on October 24, 1938, I set off from Vancouver with seven other Scarboro priests on the *Empress of Asia,* flying the Canadian flag, bound for Shanghai. There we would transship to a coastal vessel that would take us south along the coast to a small port still in Chinese hands, from which we could go up river by sampan to our destination. On board with us were eleven priests from Ireland and the United States, all members of the Columban Fathers. Most of the other passengers were Jewish refugees from Hitler's Germany whose final destination was Shanghai.

The nineteen-day voyage across the Pacific, following the Great Circle close to the Aleutian Islands, was cold and dreary. Japan, when we stopped at Yokahama, also seemed unfriendly and depressing. It was involved in war and preparing for bigger war, and the people seemed to know it. On our way south, we stopped at Kobe, then through the beautiful Inland Sea to Nagasaki, a major port with no visible inkling of the cataclysmic destruction that would rain on it from the skies just seven short years later. From there it was little more than twenty-four hours steaming across the East China Sea to the mouth of the Wangpu, which we reached at four in the morning, and where we were quickly introduced to the reality of war and the cheapness of human life in China. Our ship pushed her way toward the Shanghai docks through scores of dead bodies floating seaward in the dirty yellow water of the Yangtze and its tributaries.

That human life was abundant as well as cheap was quickly demonstrated as we neared the docks. All the people in the world seemed to be crammed into this one spot. Against a shoreline of massive Western-style buildings constructed in the imperial style of the late nineteenth century, with cupolas, clock towers, and domes, the waters teemed with sampans and rafts laden down with

merchandise and crammed with people, a scene of perpetual movement, color, and agitation, as the water
people went about their unending cycle of working, eating, sleeping, living, and dying. I began already to see
the meaning of the statistics I had put together in my
quick guide-book preparation for China. In an area
smaller than my native Canada and only slightly bigger
than the United States were packed 450 million people,
nearly a quarter of the world population. The United
States and Canada had then but 132 million and 12 million,
respectively. If only all this human energy could be con-
structively harnessed, I thought, little realizing that the
population would have grown to 760 million thirty years
later, and that by then the miracle of total mobilization
would have largely occurred.

After clearing through the Japanese customs, we waited
a week in Shanghai for a decrepit coastal vessel, flying
the Italian flag, to take us south some 500 miles to
Wenchow in Chekiang Province, which was still in Chinese hands. We had every kind of living creature on
board, pigs, chickens, ducks, geese, and—as I knew the
morning of the second day—ravenous bedbugs. But most
of all people, for all China was on the move in a frantic,
unstructured search for a place untouched by the bombs,
the carnage, and the starvation. There were hundreds
of them, and to my still unaccustomed eyes they all looked
alike, shriveled, remote, and inscrutable. Yet among
themselves the conversation was often animated, the
many-toned language adding to the impression of excitement. I felt sure that behind the masks there were human
minds that would justify the effort of getting to know
them. Here on this small ship was a whole new world
with all its concerns and activities. Even a child was
born under the stars on the open deck. I was excited
by this close-up look at the people whose souls I had

been chosen to save. I was also glad, as I looked, that I had taken the time to acquire some medical skills. I could see that they would not wither for lack of use.

At Wenchow we were the guests of Vincentian Fathers from Poland, many of whom I was to count in due course among my friends. I recall in particular a Father Viachork whose name means "evening" in Polish, and whom we usually addressed as Father Evening. He taught me how to brew beer, an accomplishment that was to prove extremely useful. For the Poles life was particularly grim, especially after Hitler, friend of the Japanese, overran their country in 1939. But they bore it all stoically. On one occasion we were talking about the food shortages in China, and Father Evening commented: "For us it's not so bad as it is for you. At home we'd be worse off than we are here."

The river was deep at Wenchow, and the men were able to use oars as we started upstream by sampan. When the water grew shallow, they poled for two days, then climbed up on the banks with ropes to pull us. When there were rapids, everyone got out and walked, and sometimes extra men were hired to pull and to carry part of the baggage. We had hired four sampans, each with four men; but as always in China, friends of the boatmen climbed aboard quite casually and stayed until we reached their destination. At night we simply pulled to the side and bedded down on our *mienbi,* with a brick for a pillow. The *mienbi,* a stuffed cotton comforter, is one's bedroll, basic equipment for every traveler.

We passed through scores of villages for which the river was the main street. Rickety houses, crowded together, jutted over its banks, and its water served for transportation, irrigation, waste disposal, and domestic use. But crowded though the villages were, they seemed not so populous as the boats and sampans that plied the waterway. Here were people who lived a life all their own, as their ancestors had lived for generations. In small space or large, they brought up their children and carried on their life, earning a living by transporting goods and passengers. The only god they worhsip is the river god. Lifetime exposure has immunized them against the diseases among which they live. They can with impunity drink the water polluted with human refuse and dead animals. As they put it, the river god knows them.

Our destination was Lishui, a city of 80,000 located a hundred miles west of Wenchow and reachable in three or four days under normal conditions. Weather and other factors could extend the time indefinitely. I remember once being overtaken by a downpour just ten miles short of Lishui and forced to pull in to the bank for the night. By morning the river was in such flood that no boat could move upstream. So we just got off and trudged the rest of the way on foot.

Lishui is in hilly country on the southern edge of the Yangtze Plain, which runs west some 600 miles from the coast in a river basin that varies in width from 20 to 200 miles. The area of the plain is 75,000 square miles, half that of California, and the population—almost all dependent on agriculture—was then some 65 million. The Yangtze Plain is in the middle in every respect in China, with Peking and the Yellow River's temperate zone to the north, and the fully tropical region of Canton to the south. Here also comes the decisive change in agriculture, from the wheat of the north to the rice of the center and south. Indeed, a large part of the Yangtze Plain enjoys two crop seasons each year, rice planted in June to be harvested by October, then a winter crop of wheat. But at Lishui on the southern edge only rice grows. What wheat enters the diet is imported from farther north.

Wheat and rice underlie the great physical differences between Chinese of the different regions of the country. Most of the overseas Chinese are from Canton, slight, low-sized, small-boned. When I got to Lishui, I was surprised to meet many six-footers, people carried south on the tide of refugees from the Yellow River where from time immemorial the diet has been wheat supplemented by kaoliang, millet, corn, sweet potatoes, and soybeans. The Lishui people themselves were neither as tall and strong as the northerners nor as small as the Cantonese, their principal diet being rice though with some wheat added. In addition, like most Chinese, the animal protein in their diet was minimal. Beef as a food was practically unknown. Little land could be spared for pasture, and consequently there were no cattle, sheep, horses, mules, or donkeys. The water buffalo or caribou and the ox, locally known as the yellow cow, were the traction animals, with human carriers to supplement the ubiquitous boats for the transport of people and merchandise. Apart from some fish, the only animal protein was supplied by pigs and chickens, both of them scavengers living on the residue of the family's meals.

Our colleagues at Lishui had prepared a great welcome for us. We were the first faces from Canada since six priests arrived just before the start of the Battle of Shanghai in 1936. Here at last was news of their families, eight strong young men to continue the work, the possibility for some of a long-delayed vacation in their own homes. So they called on the nuns to prepare a welcome banquet and they invited all the priests from the other stations to assemble at the center of Lishui. The nuns really put on a good show. They even found some canned food that had been hidden away for an emergency. It was the last good meal that any of us saw for three and a half years.

Lishui, an ecclesiastic division as big as the state of New Jersey, later became a diocese with its own bishop, but at that time it was an apostolic prefecture under the direction of the local superior of the Scarboro Fathers.

The first Catholic missionaries in Lishui were French, and they had created the organization and put up most of the buildings in which we lived. Scarboro had taken over in 1924. By now the prefecture had about twenty-five priests, all Canadians except for two Chinese and one from the United States. One Chinese priest was attached to the prefecture. The other, like all the Canadians, belonged to the Scarboro Society. We had nine sisters, Gray Nuns from Ontario. Four of them were nurses and worked in the hospital. In a population of almost 3 million, we had a total of fewer than 7,000 Catholics.

In addition to the central staff, the prefecture had ten parishes or missions, with two priests in each. The sisters had two clinics, as well as the hospital, and they conducted an orphanage and a home for old people. Most of the missions also had a school for boys.

The sisters certainly worked hard, but most of the priests had time on their hands. A typical parish had fifty to a hundred communicants, and one or two converts a year was about as much as could be anticipated. Within the framework of his self-understanding as a purveyor of the sacraments, there was literally very little for a priest to do.Besides, most of the priests had so little interest in or sensitivity for Chinese culture and life styles that they had few Chinese friends. Especially in the long rainy season, they mostly sat home and felt sorry for themselves. And, perhaps in self-defense, they quickly rationalized their idleness into virtue. I'll never forget a conversation I had with one priest, a young man who had arrived in China about two years before me. He was in charge of a boys' school and doing a fine job. I couldn't fault it. What shocked me was his philosophy.

"Here I am saving my soul," he said to me as he sat one late afternoon in a rocking chair on the verandah, fanning himself gently and swaying back and forth for relaxation. "I have left behind my family, my friends, my own culture. I am witnessing to Christ among pagans. My mere presence as a missionary is a witness, even if I never did a thing but sit here and rock on the verandah.''

"You must be kidding," I said.

"No, I'm not. I'm deadly serious." And he was. He had merely said what many of our colleagues thought. But I did not then, nor could I ever, agree. God commands man to work, to participate with him in the perfecting of the universe. And this man doesn't do sitting in a rocking chair.

Lishui was not like any city I had ever seen before. It was really an overgrown village, further swollen by refugees. You could circle it on foot in three hours. It lived off farming, and many who slept there spent their lives outside in the fields. There was no industry, not even a single high chimney that I can recall. But because of the Japanese invasion and coastal blockade, practically nothing arrived from the outside. Whatever they had was what they made with the most primitive equipment and local raw materials, things like shoes, cloth, soap, and furniture. The business section wasn't just in one place but scattered all around. Everything was a hodgepodge. With the exception of maybe a dozen families, everyone suffered the most abject poverty, strictly hand-to-mouth at a subsistence level. Compared to them, the missionaries lived like kings in their thick-walled European-style house. They all thought of us as the richest people in the city, and they were probably right.

The first order of business, of course, was to learn the language, and for this the eight newcomers were handed over to a skilled calligrapher to be instructed in the intricacies of Chinese writing and pronunciation. Mr. Lee knew no English, which made things rough at the start but which in the long run was an asset. He taught us the Mandarin of north China, which has been officially adopted as the national or standard language. One of the advantages for the beginner is that it has only four tones, whereas some of the dialects he must later master have up to eight.

Written Chinese is ideographic, which means that each word is a separate sign or "letter," so that you have to learn in effect thousands of different letters instead of the twenty-five or thirty which make up Western alphabets. An ideographic script does not fix the sound of words in the way a phonetic script does, and consequently the pronunciation changes more rapidly. All the dialects use the same ideographs and have practically the same grammatical structures. It is in the pronunciation that the major differences are found.

In ten months, studying ten hours and more each day, Mr. Lee taught us to read and pronounce about three thousand ideographs. We were still, however, far from having fully mastered the art of calligraphy. Chinese is written freehand, and it demands a reconciliation of freedom with order in such a way as to please the understanding eye which beholds it. It requires years of training with a brush rather than a pen and it normally starts at the age of six. We never became calligraphers in that sense, but most of us managed to make approximations that served the mundane purpose of transmitting information by means of a sheet of paper. Our three thousand ideographs left us still two thousand short of the number needed to read a book, newspaper, or letter intelligently. But it had brought us to a point where we could continue the process by ourselves. We accordingly began our study of the dialect that prevailed in the area of our respective assignments, and at the end of another six months we were in a position to carry on everyday conversations.

In the land of the blind, the proverb says, the one-eyed man is king. In a city without a single doctor, a man with two years of medical school and intensive courses

in first aid is the logical choice to practice medicine.
You could say I was a fully qualified quack. I knew how
to pull teeth, administer an anesthetic, set broken bones.
What more could one ask? I was consequently kept at
the mission center in Lishui and assigned to the hospital
to help the sisters as orderly and general factotum. I
was also chaplain for those who were Catholics. And
while a priest's relations with the sick and dying are not
quite the same as the work in a parish, in many ways
I was in closer contact with my "parishioners" than
would be normal out in one of our missions. I quickly
came to know a cross section of the poverty, oppression,
and degradation which was the lot of the average man,
woman, and child around me, and this experience became
one of a series of converging elements in the reappraisal
of my life purpose and of our whole approach to "the
foreign missions" which was slowly but steadily taking
shape in my mind.

Simultaneously I was being forced to the same reappraisal from a very different direction. Father Aaron Gignac had long occupied the post of procurator for the
entire mission. He was the business manager, responsible
for buying and selling, for the account books, and for
seeing that we stayed solvent. For some years past, he
had been in poor health and it was obvious that he needed
an assistant. Again my past experience singled me out.
My work back home in the family store had trained me
in the basics of buying and selling and also taught me
something about keeping books. So I began to give Father
Gignac a hand. A little later, he went down to Wenchow
where there was a hospital with a doctor, run by the
Polish priests. They operated on him, but he died a few
days later from heart failure. And so I had to take over
his job completely and soon found myself deeply entan-
gled in the internal politics of the mission.

Even before I left Canada, I already had some inkling

of what that meant. It was common knowledge among the students in the seminary that Father John McRae, the superior general in Canada, was not on the best of terms with Father William McGrath, the superior in China. We, of course, had no idea who was right and who was wrong. McGrath was halfway round the world. As for McRae, he was a fine priest, but his knowledge of China was reputedly slight. He had made two quick trips as superior, but it was said that the strange food had so complicated his life that he had time for little else.

Back in 1924, when the Scarboro Fathers accepted the China assignment, they sent out about ten men and put them under a Spanish superior, a Father Ramon Serra, in Lishui. Father Serra was picked because of his knowledge of the local situation, but he and the Canadians never learned to understand each other. There was constant misunderstanding, both within the mission and between Lishui and the headquarters in Canada. By 1931, Father McRae and his advisers had had enough, and they decided in one master stroke to solve everything, though eventually their dramatic solution solved nothing. They cabled a thirty-five-year-old priest on the high seas to tell him that when he landed in China he would be in full charge.

Father William C. McGrath was a Newfoundland Irishman who had been ordained for the diocese of St. John in 1921 and had joined Scarboro in 1925, when it was only eight years in existence and still consisted of just two priests, Father McRae and one other. McGrath was a brilliant man and he quickly developed into a kind of public relations man for the Society. He was a wonderful talker, completely in command on a platform, and with a beautiful sense of humor. He also edited a small magazine.

Whether or not McRae and his council had decided

to name McGrath superior when they assigned him to China in 1931, I never did discover. In any case, they notified him only after he had sailed. And it did not take him long after he arrived before he discovered they had done him no favor. He was starting dead cold, without the language, without specialized training in mission methods or the experience that would enable him to evaluate the level of performance of his colleagues. Several of the ten priests were much older than he was, and apparently some were miffed at the idea of having a novice tell them how to do their jobs. In time, of course, Father McGrath did learn some Chinese, but he never succeeded in breaking down the barrier between him and the others. To ease the monotony of his isolation, he would make frequent trips to Shanghai, staying with the Jesuits in the International Settlement. Even after the Japanese occupation, foreigners remained relatively unmolested. Meanwhile, he was apparently less than garrulous in the reports he had to send back periodically to Canada, presumably hoping that ultimately things would straighten themselves out. And at that level, I had considerable sympathy with him. I learned in due course that one of the biggest problems of the China mission was the refusal back home to recognize the need for any adjustment of life style or approach to evangelization, even when we were all caught up in a galloping inflation and a major war.

Father McRae brought me directly into the conflict just before I left Canada. While I was waiting to board the train at Toronto, he buttonholed me, poured out his problems, and importuned me to give him a full report on what McGrath was up to. There was no particular reason why he should have selected me to act as his investigator. I suppose he decided that I was not only the oldest but the most experienced in the ways of the world. I had no intention of starting my career in China as an undercover agent, but naturally all I could do was to listen sympathetically and promise to keep eyes and ears open.

I had scarcely reached Lishui when I was attacked from the other side. The first official act was a welcome to the newcomers in the cathedral. As prefect apostolic, McGrath dressed like a bishop and wore a pectoral cross, and in the pulpit he was still able to impress his audience. After the liturgical ceremony we had the banquet I already mentioned, and by nine o'clock it was bedtime.

Early next morning, McGrath knocked on my door and invited me to his room, where for four hours he cross-examined me about the situation back at headquarters in Canada. "What are those men trying to do to me?" he demanded over and over again, as he ransacked his files for their letters and cables. All I could do was plead ignorance, explaining that I had worked in a parish a long way from headquarters from the time I was ordained, and that I knew less about the inner workings than he did.

I was really embarrassed when I arrived with McGrath for the midday meal after that long session. I had told some of the others about McRae's request in Toronto, and I could now sense what they were thinking: that Steele knew how to work both sides of the street. Here he was, the white-haired boy, only twenty-four hours on deck, and already closeted all morning with the superior. The mortification added to my annoyance with both McRae and McGrath, both of whom seemed to want to keep their own hands clean and leave me to do their dirty work for them. I found myself asking once again if this was how churchmen always exercised their authority; and if so, how long I could continue to tolerate it. McGrath shortly freed me of the need to answer the question at that time by taking off again for Shanghai. He left at five one morning without telling a soul. By pure chance, I saw him as I went over to the cathedral to say the early Mass. He was waiting for a rickshaw to take him to the bus station, no doubt with the intention of riding a bus to Ningpo and picking up a coastal steamer to Shanghai. He got a job on a small English-language radio station in Shanghai and never came back to Lishui. I saw him again shortly before his death in 1970. He had returned to Canada before Pearl Harbor, later moved south to the United States where the devotion to Our Lady of Fatima, with overtones of anticommunism that appealed to many of the old China hands, was becoming popular. It attracted him and he stayed with it the rest of his working life, returning to Scarboro to retire shortly before he died. When I saw him there, he was a broken man, and I can agree with those who subsequently told me that he died because he had lost the will to live.

If Father McGrath's departure from Lishui removed one problem for me, it created another. He left behind him in charge of the prefecture a Father Leo Curtin, an old man who was almost stone deaf. Father Curtin had been a pastor in Ottawa for twenty years before coming to Scarboro, and he had been sent to China without any realization that the combination of age and deafness excluded any possibility of learning Chinese. He was a very fine, decent person but completely unrelated to what was happening around him. When the Japanese would send in a flight of bombers and the ground all around was trembling from the explosions, he would look up with mild surprise and ask what was going on. Later, when he began to realize what was in fact going on, he simply lost his nerve and refused to make any decisions. To aggravate his condition, he was plagued with malaria, which, for lack of effective medications, had reached the final stage of invasion of the cerebral tissues.

Curtin's progressive incapacitation left the prefecture without an effective canonical superior, so that people tended to turn to me as the procurator for decisions. It had always been the tradition in China to treat the procurator as the number two man. Some of the older priests understandably resented my growing importance in the hierarchy. I sympathized with them, but there was literally nothing I could do about it. Communications had been effectively broken by the Japanese both with McGrath and McRae.

Two Views of Chinese Culture

A parallel development was also gradually opening another breach between me and many of my colleagues. Although Father Gignac was in poor health when I was assigned to help him in his work as procurator, I soon learned that his mind was keen. He had twenty or more volumes of English translations of St. Thomas Aquinas, and I conceived the idea—which he gladly accepted—that the two of us should work our way through them together, each in turn preparing lessons. In the seminary, theology had been a chore. Now it came alive. I learned more from Father Gignac in the eighteen months before he died than in all my formal studies. For our colleagues, whose intellectual interests were limited to cards, dominoes, and pool, such waste of time bordered on lunacy.

Father Gignac was interested not only in St. Thomas but in China. He had an outstanding command of the language and he respected the people and their customs. He was a friend of Father Desmond Stringer, whom I had once met briefly when he was back in Canada on vacation. He said that Stringer knew more Chinese than any other foreigner around. Stringer was unique in that he had a fairly good library of books dealing with China and its culture. It was there I read for the first time about the sixteenth-century mission of the Jesuit Matteo

Ricci to China where he steeped himself so thoroughly in Chinese language, literature, and customs that he adopted Chinese dress and was made court mathematician and astronomer at Peking. When we reached China, we had to take an oath in the cathedral never to discuss the Chinese Rites. None of us knew what they were, nor thought the issue important enough to ask. The bishops had met in Shanghai in 1924 and made the rule. We did what we were told. In Stringer's library I learned that the Chinese Rites were an adaptation by Ricci and his companions of Catholic practice to Chinese culture, and that Rome had condemned them in the seventeenth century, after a long series of vacillations, for reasons that had little or no bearing on their orthodoxy or value. The more I learned about them, the more I became convinced that a major part of the blame of Christianity's failure ever to make an impact on China lay at the door of Rome's legalistic officials.

To voice such views to our colleagues would have been suicidal. As I was to discover later, Father Gignac and I were not the first missionaries to question the wisdom of identifying Christianity with Western culture and to think that the Chinese had much to teach us. There was, for example, Father Frederick Lebbe, a Vincentian from Belgium known in his order as Father Vincent. He had been in China since 1901, had become a naturalized Chinese, and assumed the Chinese name of Lei-Ming Yuan. He wore his hair in a pigtail, dressed like a Buddhist priest, and identified himself emotionally with the Chinese people in all respects. He had great influence with Chiang Kai-shek and other Chinese leaders up to his death in 1940 in Chungking. But few of my colleagues or the other missionaries knew anything about him, and those who did refused to take him seriously. The correct attitude for the missionary, they were persuaded, was laid down in the decrees of Rome and the

almost unbroken tradition of all the missionaries from
the West. Even to show respect for Chinese customs
and a desire to adapt to Chinese social attitudes quickly
evoked a response of uneasiness. We were all uncon-
scious cultural imperialists. We were convinced that we
had done our part by simply transferring ourselves to
this strange land and presenting ourselves as ready to
share the spiritual treasures entrusted to us by the Lord.
To sit and rock on a Chinese verandah was already a
major fulfilment of our duty. Any heathen who couldn't
understand this and respond appropriately was simply
in bondage to the devil and culpably rejecting the offered
grace.

As I took over more of Father Gignac's work and
developed links with the many Chinese with whom I
bought, sold, and bartered to keep the mission going,
I gradually came to see how inadequate was such an
evaluation. The Chinese themselves had made an enormously different analysis of these same facts, and the more
I learned of their views, the more difficult it became
to deny their validity.

An old carpenter with whom I frequently dealt when
I wanted a chair or table made, or any odd job done
around the house, one day formulated for me his side
of the story. His name was Lee, the same name as my
language teacher and many other Chinese, and he lived
and worked in a little compound next door to our big
building. From my washroom I could look down and
see him in his patio. The design of the Chinese house
is remarkably consistent in all parts of the country and
has changed little for centuries. It has a main entrance
defended on the inside by a spirit screen which blocks
the inside courtyard or patio from view. Since Chinese
demons can move only in straight lines, this screen provides total protection. The home was originally planned
as the common dwelling place of the branches of a large

family, each with its own courtyard, but people of modest means like Mr. Lee, the carpenter, had to be content with a single unit.

Mr. Lee was about sixty. As a native of Chekiang Province, he was bigger than the typical Cantonese but stockier than the normal Westerner. He had a very friendly face. The smile was just under the surface, but it was always there. Chinese usually retain their natural hair color until they get bald, but he was quite gray and still had all his hair. He was a good man, known to the community as absolutely honest. A devout Buddhist, he would frequently worship his household gods by going down on his knees before their images on the patio and burning joss sticks for them. He had a wife and children, and I think also a second wife, a "little wife," as the expression was. Anyone who could afford it took a second wife as a matter of course. There was no moral stigma attached. And Mr. Lee could afford it. Although the town had a dozen carpenter shops, he was always busy and normally employed three or four helpers.

From my washroom I would watch Mr. Lee burn his joss sticks, and I would wonder why he clung to his superstitions while he lived in the shadow of the true religion. Mr. Wong, our catechist, had a booming voice, and he was constantly instructing someone who sought baptism. There was probably no Christian in Lishui as well versed in the truths of faith as Mr. Lee, who had been listening uninterruptedly to Mr. Wong's harangues not only since the Scarboro Fathers arrived but away back in the time of the French priests.

One day I challenged Mr. Lee. His innate courtesy kept him from laughing outright, but the submerged smile rose perceptibly toward the surface. "Your religion," he told me, "has no relevance for us. Those who join you are our morally least reputable citizens. They are what you yourselves call rice Christians. They want a job, free medicine, or free schooling for their children.''

On the issue of doctrine, Mr. Lee was equally challenging. ''Sex is the one enjoyment of the poor, who are 90 percent of our people. It makes their dreary lives tolerable... you tell them it is a sin. And to make matters worse, you say there will not be sex in paradise either. We are realists. You have nothing to offer that we want. Our own myths make a lot more sense than yours do. Now, if you could create an alternative, if you could offer the poor some escape from their misery, then perhaps they would have the leisure and the understanding to reflect. Perhaps they would come to find something worthwhile in your message. But right now, all we see is where we are. And you have nothing to say that we can hear.''

I found it difficult to believe that all ''our Christians,'' as we used to call them, were as mercenary as he claimed, although I had to recognize that conversion had not produced any startling changes that would cause them to stand out as morally superior to their neighbors. But a concrete test occurred not too long afterwards, when the Japanese were on our doorstep and we needed friends to save our lives. In that crisis, only one man among all of Lishui's Christians was willing to risk his own welfare in order to defend us. He was a small merchant from whom I bought salt and charcoal. Knowing how near the Japanese were, he exposed himself by coming and urging me to get everyone out. ''If the Sisters are here another twenty-four hours,'' he said, ''they will all be raped.''

There was another point in Mr. Lee's bill of particulars which I could not challenge, namely, that we lived at such a remove from the Chinese that we could never hope to establish true human understanding and compasion with them. It is a problem which faces every missionary coming from a more developed country to a poor one, a problem about which a greater number of missionaries are becoming conscious, but for which few find a satisfactory solution. "You are rich by every Chinese standard," he said. "You have a big compound, servants, good food, electric light. When you are sick, you are taken away to a hospital. When you are weary, you go back to your homes for a vacation."

All this was true, and yet from our point of view we were close to destitute. The food was particularly unsatisfactory. For three years we didn't have a drop of milk. I should rather say that the only milk one could obtain was human milk, as I discovered when I interrogated Mr. Wong, our catechist, about a lady who visited him each day. He was embarrassed but finally explained. She was a mother who had killed her female child, as was common, and was selling him a quart of milk daily for a tuberculous condition. The Chinese believed that no medicine was as potent and versatile as a mother's milk. The only meat available was a little chicken and pork, usually served undercooked because of the scarcity of fuel. And when we saw how the pigs and chickens lived on the refuse of homes in which most of the people were tuberculous, syphilitic, and worm-infected, we ate this meat with fear and nausea. Even the chicken wasn't like anything to which we were accustomed, most of it being black meat of a kind I have never in my life seen anywhere else. Rice and vegetables formed the rest of the diet; and apart from carrots and occasional beans, all the vegetables were varieties unknown to the West, and to our palates utterly tasteless.

The rest of our lives were very much on the same level. We improvised as best we could. The Polish priests in Wenchow had laid in a big stock of imported hops which they shared with us, and under the guidance of the good Father Evening, I became a tolerable brewmaster. We also made candles and soap, and we used peanut butter instead of regular butter. As the Japanese blockade tightened, we used the leaves of certain trees to substitute for tobacco and rolled our own cigarettes. The town had electric light for those who could afford it, and kerosene had been stockpiled so that the plant could function for three or four hours each evening. That also meant that we could use our radio, one of the few in town, tuning in to a BBC English-language broadcast that kept us abreast of world events. Most of the time, we didn't even have a shower, although we improvised one toward the end. Before that, all we had was a basin of water which we splashed over us. It got quite cold for a couple of months in the winter, and then you heated up water on the stove in your room about once every two weeks and washed yourself. Even for someone raised on a farm in Nova Scotia, it was primitive.

Still there was no denying that it was luxury compared to what was all around us. The people lived in the most miserable shacks, without beds or furniture, open to the elements because the climate was tropical most of the year, hot and clammy. But in the winter the temperature dropped at times to freezing. So all the people could do was wrap themselves in layers of dirty cloth, which they wore day and night. When the weather grew warmer in spring, they would strip down again. I used to watch our old gateman in April, when the sun was getting strong. He would start about ten o'clock in the morning to peel off his layers one by one, seven or eight of them in all. And as each layer of cloth came down, he would methodically kill the lice that clung to it, the thousands of them who had lived on him through the winter, for of course he never took a bath.

Everywhere I went about Lishui on my errands as business manager for the mission, the message was the same. There was no challenging the correctness of Mr. Lee's analysis. Here were people who had absolutely no control over their lives. They were poor beyond anything I could imagine, and they lived within a system which ensured that they would always remain poor because it siphoned off the benefit of their work. They were slaves. If a man's father had been a water carrier, then he had no choice but to be a water carrier. Even to move up to be a rickshaw driver was practically impossible. Social stability was maintained by keeping everyone in his place. These were the most intelligent people in the world, but because they couldn't read or write they were totally dependent on the few who could. And the more I learned about the details of their destitution, the more I came to understand the width of the gap between us. For me, there was always an escape. For them and for their children, there was no escape so long as the system enslaved them. If we were ever to meet as humans, if we were ever to talk together about God and mean the same thing, it could be only after they had broken out of their enslavement. That, Mr. Lee taught me, had to come first. Later, we might get to doctrinal luxuries.

Desirable as social change might be, however, my growing knowledge of Chinese thought processes and attitudes made me realize that no foreigner could exercise any significant leadership role. The Chinese had an understandable prejudice against all of us. They found our customs far less civilized than their own. And several hundred years of association had brought them nothing but indignities and losses. They knew from experience that we were inveterate breakers of our word. Even the hands of the missionaries were far from clean. Or, at least from the viewpoint of the Chinese, the missionary had always brought the trader, and the trader was quickly followed by the gunboat.

At this particular time, there were more imperious reasons to prevent any exploration of the possibility of social change. The impact of the Japanese occupation of the territories to the north of us had become total. Absolutely nothing was coming through the blockade. Inflation was out of hand. And the aerial bombardments were growing in frequency and intensity. To get together a little food occupied one's entire time. All that worried people was to stay alive until tomorrow.

The Japanese bombing was something we had to learn to live with almost from the beginning of our stay. The only time we were really free of bombings was during the monsoon rains when the airplanes couldn't operate. At other times we would have many bombings in a single day or night. There was no organized defense. A huge temple bell was rung as a warning if planes approached, and the nearer they came the faster it tolled. What the Japanese were really doing at first was to train pilots for their later attacks on Singapore and Hong Kong after Pearl Harbor. A plane would drop a bomb in the direction of a particular building, then circle again and again until it was finally hit. Bombs were usually not dropped in bunches, but one at a time and with great economy. Although the city was swarming with soldiers, they had no antiaircraft guns and simply rushed for shelter like everyone else. China had an estimated 20 million conscripts, but there was only one gun per hundred soldiers. All that identified the soldier was his green tunic and pants. Like the civilian, he went barefoot or wore sandals made from old auto tires or straw.

Long Flight to Chungking

The tempo of the attacks shot up in April 1942 when Tokyo was bombed by American planes under General Doolittle flying from the carrier *Hornet*. We were in the part of China not under Japanese domination which was closest to Japan, and the Americans had made arrangements with the Chinese government to have the raiders land at the military airbase at Lishui after dropping their bombs. In fact, a big building to house the pilots was constructed at the airbase, and it was said that the intention was to set up a shuttle and bomb the Japanese homeland constantly. Apparently the Japanese had some knowledge of the plan, because many of the Chinese had sold out to them. In any case, they were able to prevent its execution. We saw the planes come in from the north from the direction of Tokyo. They came in the evening just after dark, flying at treetop level. But the lights to guide them to the airfield were not switched on, whether through treachery or just plain bungling it was never established. Two of the raiders reached Russian territory away up north and three came down in places occupied by the Japanese, but several crashed in friendly country near us, and subsequently we met some of the men.

The Japanese were furious not only at the military threat but also at the insult. They had promised their people that no foreign attack would ever reach their homeland. Immediately they set out to eliminate the offending base at Lishui, and we were treated to an incredible aerial display as the divebombers zeroed in on the building intended for the Americans. The city itself also took a terrible pounding. Bodies lay in the streets, impaled on poles, strung up on electric wires, literally thousands of them. All we did was to keep running from the bombs. When the weather was fine, everyone able to walk would leave the city in the early morning to hide in the hills until dusk. It was real hell. We would lie on our bellies for hours with the bombs falling around us, until finally the nervous system of many people broke down and they would pray to die. Some of the nuns, two of them especially, went hysterical for a long time, and there was nothing we could do for them. There was little food and no medicine, and not a doctor within hundreds of miles. The Japanese let us know that Lishui was being punished for the help it had planned to give the Americans and threatened worse things for any repetition. And they lived up to that threat. When they learned that an injured American pilot had been operated on at a church hospital at Nanchang, the diocese of Irish Columban Bishop Patrick Cleary in Kiangsi Province which adjoined us to the southwest, they sent in planes to demolish the hospital, dropping leaflets at the same time to explain the reason.

For double security, the Japanese shortly decided that they should wipe out the last pockets of Chinese resistance in the entire coastal region in which future American raiders might find sanctuary. By the summer of 1942 the radio was warning that we could soon expect a major offensive. The rumors and the uncertainties were building up explosively. The soldiers were said to have gotten completely out of hand when they occupied Nanking, raping 800,000 women. And word had come through to us from the apostolic delegate in Peking which was in Japanese-held territory, that no nationals of countries at war with Japan should be allowed to fall into Japanese hands.

I tried to get Father Curtin to realize the gravity of the situation and give the appropriate orders. But the poor man had lost all contact with reality. We had gotten a small amount of quinine, enough to keep him alive but not even enough to get his temperature down. Then Sister Juliet appealed to me. At first I urged her to talk to Father Curtin, but when she said she could get no guidance from him, I advised her to try to find a boat for her five companions and herself. As for me, I told her, I was taking off on my bicycle at noon. That was

nine o'clock in the morning. It was August 1942, and
the Japanese were already on the outskirts of Lishui.
Had we waited another twenty-four hours, we would
all certainly have been trapped. But we joined the tens
of thousands of refugees streaming south, I on my bicycle,
the nuns in a boat they had managed to get from a friendly
Chinese family, all the other priests—including poor
Father Curtin—by sampan, bicycle, or on foot.

The most southerly Scarboro mission was at
Lungchuan and we decided to rendezvous there. We
traveled alone or in small groups, sleeping where we
could, eating as we found food to beg or buy. The road
through the mountains was rugged and the midsummer
weather was hot and humid. But fear is a powerful spur,
and I covered the hundred miles on my bicycle in a little
over two days. It took closer to two months for all the
others to make their way from their various missions,
but finally the entire Scarboro group of twenty-three
priests and nuns was together at Lungchuan. I still had
some money, but the place was so crowded with refugees
that the food supplies were practically exhausted, raising
prices so rapidly that money became valueless. So it was
agreed that we would split up evenly what little money
I was still holding as business manager, and that we should
strike out for Kweilin in Kwangsi Province, several
hundred miles further south and still considered safe.
The church there was headed by Monsignor John
Romaniello, a Maryknoller from the United States, and
he undoubtedly would have work for all comers.

I left Lungchuan on a truck headed south into Fukien
Province, then traveled west to Kanchow in Kiangsi
Province. The truck was owned by the government, and
its cargo included the provincial mint of Chekiang. Under
the Chinese system, the provinces had a wide autonomy.
Each minted its own coins and collected customs duties
at its borders, even on the produce of neighboring prov-

inces. While moving through Fukien Province, we were guests first of the Dominican Fathers from New York, then of German and of Spanish missionaries. At Kanchow we stayed with the Vincentian Fathers from Germantown, Pennsylvania. They included Bishop O'Shea, Father Daniel McGillicuddy, Father Ken Williams, and Father Fred Maguire. It was the first of many meetings with Father Maguire, who today is director of the Latin America Bureau of the United States Catholic Conference, in Washington, D.C. The Vincentians had started their work in China in 1924, the same year that the Scarboro Fathers had arrived in the country. Their mission headquarters at Kanchow had been occupied by Mao Tse-tung in 1927 during the Great March of the Seventh Army from Kwantung Province diagonally across China to Yennan in the extreme northwest. While occupying Bishop O'Shea's home, Mao's soldiers planted hedges and flower beds that were still there in 1942. In Yennan they recouped their strength and built the power base which ultimately enabled them to survive the Japanese invasion and then defeat Chiang Kai-shek.

Before we left Lungchuan, it had been agreed that Father Alec McIntosh and I should continue on to Chungking, where Chiang Kai-shek had set up his capital. Through the Swiss Embassy there we would be able to contact our home-base in Canada and get some desperately needed money. However, I had lost contact with Father McIntosh somewhere on the road, and I decided to continue alone. Fortunately, Monsignor Romaniello was friendly with some of the famous Flying Tigers, who carried supplies and arms across the Hump from Burma and India to landing strips in various parts of China, and they gave me a ride—my first air trip—a thousand miles west to Kunming in Yannan Province. From there I hitchhiked for two months by truck west and north in a wide arc of a circle almost to the foothills of the

Tibetan mountains. Here the dialects were so totally different from everything I knew that it was only by writing the characters I could make people understand that I wanted food. Finally we reached the Yangtze far above Chungking and I fought my way aboard a river boat. There were a thousand of us in a space intended for a hundred, packed so tight together that for three days and nights I was literally unable to lie down to rest. The best one could do was to squat. Up to then I had been lucky while traveling through bandit-infested country, having had two narrow shaves but always escaping without loss. In the mob on the boat, however, my luck turned. I was robbed of every remaining penny I had left, not very much but enough to buy my food. I would have starved were it not for a young couple, Chinese refugees from Shanghai, who shared their food with me and gave me money to pay for a rickshaw on arrival.

Chiang Kai-shek had picked Chungking as temporary capital in 1937 mainly because distance made it safe from the Japanese threat. It is 1,500 miles up the Yangtze, at the confluence of the Kialing, and it is built on a rock promontory, so that all suppplies must be carried up from the river front by stairways or inclined railroad. An industrial city of a more than a million and a half people, it had cotton and silk mills, chemical plants, and some steel and cement production. But the trade that was really flourishing when I got there was espionage. During World War II the city shared with Lisbon the reputation of having the greatest number of agents, counter agents, and double agents. I learned shortly from Father Mark Tennien, a Maryknoller, who gave me a place to eat and sleep, that here were located the brains behind the black market in currency and the big-time beneficiaries. The actual transactions of this black market, I also learned, took place in Kunming from which I had come and where I was shortly to return.

Father Tennien, my host and guide, was a fine person, a learned man, and the author of several books. But he was too progressive in his outlook for his time, questioning the value of much of the mission work in China, and he never became a bishop. We were joined by an Irishman, Father Edward McManus, sent by Bishop Patrick Cleary of Nanchang, and by Father Teddy Bauman, a Society of the Divine Word priest from Youngstown, Ohio. All of us had the same job, to get whatever dollars we could get through the Swiss Embassy from our respective mother houses and convert them into yen in order to keep our colleagues alive and maintain the mission activities to the extent the war permitted.

It was a fixed policy of Chiang Kai-shek's government to maintain the official exchange rate of sixteen yen to the dollar. As inflation grew and prices rose, we got less and less for our dollars. It had been a constant source of friction between us in Lishui and our Canadian headquarters. They blamed my lack of administrative know-how for the constantly higher numbers of dollars we needed in order to survive miserably. We could never get across to them the fact of galloping inflation combined with a fixed exchange rate. Indeed at the end, we had reached a point where a pack of cigarettes was worth more than a suitcase packed with yen notes. It was like Germany after the First World War! The paper in the note was worth more than the face value.

What neither the people in Canada nor I knew until Father Tennien explained it to me was that nobody sold dollars at the official exchange any more. Instead, there was a flourishing black market manipulated by Harvard-educated T. V. Soong, Chiang Kai-shek's finance minister and reputedly the richest man in China. Also in Chungking and equally implicated were Soong's three sisters, one the widow of Sun Yat-sen, China's first major Marxist leader, the second the wife of Moscow-trained Chiang

Kai-shek whom she had married just about the time he broke with the Communists in 1927, and the third married to the Minister of State H.H. Kung. The physical transactions of currency exchange were centered at Kunming. It was the Chinese city closest to the Indian border and also the terminus of the Burma Road. The Chinese merchants exchanged their yen there for Indian rupees so that they could cross into India, buy medicines and other supplies, and smuggle them back into China. So the real business was to exchange dollars for rupees in India, then exchange the rupees for yen in Kunming. In that way one ended up with several thousand yen for a dollar instead of sixteen.

Father Tennien also told me of a policy decision that had been made by the twenty or twenty-five Catholic bishops whose dioceses were in unoccupied China. When the inflation had reached uncontrollable levels, the Protestants had handed over hospitals, schools, and other property to local groups in each city, deciding that they would have the best chance to keep them going. The Catholic bishops, however, felt that they should hang on to the bitter end and show their commitment for life to their churches by maintaining what they could, even if that meant acquiring yen in the black market the way the Chinese leaders themselves were doing.

Although a much bigger city than Lishui, Chungking had the same high proportion of poverty. Chinese cities are always crowded, but the war had added vast numbers of refugees to the normal population. The slopes leading to the river were crowded with tiny wooden houses and shops, joined by narrow passages, with more rickety houses arching over the passages. Masses of people moved back and forth like ants at all hours of the day and night. Hundreds of water carriers struggled up the steps, each with wooden buckets balanced on a bamboo pole. Other hundreds of porters carried bales of merchandise or people in sedan chairs. In the city above, the wide main street was chock full of buses, cars, taxis, rickshaws, and sedan chairs, and the pavements were equally full of pedestrians. Life went on publicly to the accompaniment of indescribable noise. A traveling restaurant consisted of a bamboo pole with a stove, bowl, and serving dishes at one end and several containers of food at the other. The restaurateur made his bargain with a passer-by and placed his wares on the ground. The customer squatted in front of the stove, took a bowl of rice, and served himself with chopsticks to the agreed number of morsels from the food containers. People wandered along the street carrying a single article for sale raised high on a bamboo pole. A barber banged two pieces of metal to signify that he was open for business. Everyone seemed to have a crude bell or drum to advertise his wares or services. On all sides one saw cats, with collars around their necks, chained to a post. The city swarmed with rats, and as the rats preyed on the silkworms which everyone kept, there was always a big demand for cats to hunt the rats.

Up on Embassy Row, as we called our street, life was different. The American, English, and French embassies were near us, and we got to know many of their people, as well as Chinese officials. We would go to eat with them and they would come to us. Even Finance Minister Soong dined at our place a couple of times, as I recalled in 1971 when he choked to death in California on a chicken bone. I was living better than I had ever lived in China, although I must say that the conditions in the homes of the American priests I had encountered on my great trek to Chungking were vastly superior to our life style in Lishui. They had more money than the Canadians and they were much better supplied with the necessities and comforts of Western life.

An event occurred in 1943 which made it possible for

me to return to Kunming and thus facilitate my currency transactions. The previous year, General Joseph Stilwell, an old China hand and for a time Chiang Kai-shek's chief of staff, had been forced by the Japanese to retreat through the Burma jungles into India. But he quickly regrouped his forces, and before long he was back in the China-Burma border region with a quarter of a million Americans under his command. There was an acute shortage of chaplains, and I undertook to join them, first on a part-time and later on a full-time basis. I was assigned to an Air Force base near the Indochina border, and I had a jeep to take me into Kunming and transact my business. Several times I also got over into India, sometimes in Air Force planes, sometimes on commercial flights. We had set up accounts in different banks in Calcutta, and we would take money belts and move a million-dollars worth of rupees in a single run.

In Calcutta I usually stayed at the Sacred Heart rectory, which was the central house for the Jesuits in southeast India. That was where I first heard of a Belgian Jesuit who had worked in this area and acquired the reputation of being the greatest missionary since St. Francis Xavier. His name was Constant Lievens, and the primacy he gave to social justice in his missionary approach appealed to me instantly. Father Lievens had lived in Calcutta from 1880 to 1885, then went to the district of Chota-Nagpur, three hundred miles distant, and established his headquarters in the town of Ranchi. The people who lived in the surrounding jungles were extremely poor, victims not only of ignorance but of exploitation by loansharks, landlords, and unscrupulous policemen. Father Lievens soon discovered that they were losing their land to the loansharks, who were paying graft to the police in order to secure their support. He began to study the land laws and soon was in a position to vindicate the rights of the poor in the lawcourts. His fame spread far and wide, so that entire villages would come to him with their title deeds, and it was not unusual for him to spend a whole night with the people examining titles and clarifying problems. His patience in these activities and his obvious love for the people quickly won them over. In his first year, 2,500 of them became Christians, and in five years the number grew to 80,000. His enormous energy soon overtaxed his strength and he fell ill. His superiors sent him back home to Belgium to recuperate, but it was too late. He died there before reaching the age of forty. Another Belgian Jesuit, a former classmate named Hoffman, took over where Father Lievens left off. He introduced credit unions and cooperatives to the whole area, thus gradually eliminating the exploitation of the people by the loansharks and merchants. Simultaneously, Christianity prospered so strikingly that in 1912 Ranchi was made a diocese with more than 300,000 Christian inhabitants.

Life as an Air Force chaplain was a delightful experience after all I had been through. It was my first meeting with Americans in substantial numbers. My only previous contacts had been during short visits to Boston or New York. Here they were from all parts of the United States, and they made a most favorable impression on me. They were running constant raids on the ports of Haiphong (Vietnam) and Hong Kong, both of which were then major Japanese bases, and their casualties were heavy. But their spirit was tremendous. One thing that struck me was the extraordinary variation of their reactions when they themselves experienced bombing. At times there were heavy Japanese raids, though nothing like it had been at tree-top level in undefended Lishui. When the bombs began to explode, some would lose all control of themselves, hiding in absurd places which gave absolutely no protection. Others were perfectly calm and nonchalant. The wide range of emotional expression fascinated me after my many years among the Chinese for whom the violent expression of one's feelings is unforgivable.

Chinese attitudes and practices were, of course, a source of unending amazement for the troops who had arrived with no preparation for this very different culture. I will never forget, for example, the shock experienced one day by Father Joe McNamara of Providence, Rhode Island, who was chief chaplain for the CBI (China-Burma-India) Theater. Joe had come into Chungking to see if he could recruit some of the refugee missionaries as army chaplains. There was an estimated quarter of a million GIs in China at the time and they had hardly any Catholic chaplains. I had agreed to go with him full-time provided he could find me a location where I could send and receive cables. He attached me to the Fourteenth Air Force at a base about twenty miles from Kunming. Joe was a much older man than I was and he had no previous experience of China. The two of us went out walking one Sunday and after a while we took to a path in the rice fields to get away from the dust being raised on the road by passing jeeps. The path gradually narrowed down until finally we found ourselves walking in single file. Off in the distance in front of us I saw six or eight dogs. I recognized them immediately as *wonks*. These wonks, as they were called, were scavengers who run wild in packs, living on all kinds of garbage and filth. I noticed that two or three of them ran off when they saw us, and I told Joe that if we went farther, we would soon find a dead body. "How do you know that?" he asked. "Didn't you see those dogs slink off with their tails between their legs?" I answered. "That's a giveaway. The Chinese don't bury their dead in the ground. They just put the coffin on top of the ground, with a few stones and some earth on top of it, or possibly nothing at all. So the dogs know this and they track down the place and feast on the human remains. But the extraordinary thing is that these dogs behave as though they had guilt feelings. If a live person approaches when they are attacking a corpse, they slink away as you saw them doing." Joe refused to believe and we continued on for a hundred yards. By that time the rest of the pack had retreated in the same cowed way as the others, and the stench of the rotting flesh convinced Joe that I had been right. For me the sight was a quite common one, for millions of dogs in China lived off such corpses. I always found it strange that the Chinese have such veneration for their ancestors and yet human life is cheap. They throw female babies away without compunction, and the body of a stranger merits no consideration.

I was perfectly content to stay on in China as a chaplain in the Air Force for as long as I might be needed, but my superiors back in Canada were insisting that I should come home. The erosion of our base in China as a result of the long war with Japan had caused a real crisis at the headquarters of the Scarboro Society in Canada, and the prospects that things would improve after the defeat of Japan were not bright. The entire membership of the Society was no more than eighty and our only mission had been China up to the early 1940's, when a dozen men were sent to Santo Domingo in the Caribbean at the request of the Holy See. Reports trickling back to Canada indicated that most of the priests in China were very unhappy with their experience and were thinking of leaving the Society as soon as they got home. Those reports were, in fact, well founded. Many of my colleagues made no secret of their intention to go back to their original dioceses once they got out of China, and several of them did so when they reached Canada. They were unhappy with what they regarded as mismanagement of the mission by the superiors in Canada, with the unreasonableness of the expectation and demands made by men who had little understanding of the circumstances of our lives, and with their consistently bad choice of local superiors for the China mission. I agreed with the others on these matters, and I also had some additional reasons of my own.

Ultimately, what I was questioning in my own mind was the whole theological basis of our approach to bringing Christianity to the masses of Chinese living in subhuman poverty, or indeed to people in any country living in similar conditions. As Mr. Lee, the carpenter, had expressed it to me back in Lishui, our message of salvation presented to them in the way we were doing it made no sense to them. One had only to look at the record of Christian effort to realize that. Ever since the time of St. Francis Xavier in the middle of the sixteenth century, there had been almost continuous missionary efforts, massive at many times. Tens of thousands of priests, brothers, and nuns from many nations had given their lives, many of them literally dying as martyrs. There was no end to the cost and the effort, but the results were infinitesimal. At the most optimistic calculation, far less than 1 percent of the Chinese people had embraced Christianity, and I had demonstrated for myself that Mr. Lee was right when he said that many of the converts were rice Catholics and people of low moral character. In the extreme north of China and also in the extreme south there were substantial numbers of first-class Catholics, quite different in the opinion of Sinologists from those in the central areas both east and west. I have never found a reasonable explanation for this admitted contrast. I have wondered whether there is not a difference in the human quality of the people, or perhaps there was a different missionary approach.

Mr. Lee's conclusions were further reinforced by a very extraordinary man with whom I established a deep friendship in Chungking, Stanley Smith, an Australian who was in charge of British information services in

China. Stanley had had a checkered career. He had been one of Australia's top Communists in the early 1920's, broke with the party, went to the United States and obtained a Ph.D. in psychology, then returned to Australia to work as a newspaperman. He met his first Catholic bishop when he interviewed the famous Archbishop Daniel Mannix of Melbourne. Mannix made a lasting impression on him, giving him an appreciation of the enormous potential for social development available to the Church. "If only you Catholics would put your mind to it," he would say to me, "you could steal the thunder of the Communists by taking the leadership in the reform of society." He was excited by what I told him of the cooperative movement developed by priests in Canada's Maritime Provinces, and he approved wholeheartedly of my idea of carrying this movement into the backward countries and territories of the world.

Stanley knew many of the top world leaders personally. Anthony Eden had brought him to England to advise the Churchill government in its dealings with the Russians, and he had been present when Churchill met Roosevelt in Quebec and when the two of them met Stalin in Teheran. As a result of these meetings and of his earlier experience in the Communist party, he was convinced that the great danger to the postwar world would be the aggressive expansion of Soviet communism. In this respect, as he once told me after staying up several nights listening to the German radio, he agreed with Hitler. While he admired Churchill and Roosevelt, he felt that their judgment at the Big Four meetings was unduly affected by narrow political concerns. "Not one of them could hold a candle to Mannix," he once told me. "What a shame that he wastes his talents in a sacristy! If only the Church with its organized network of talented men would go to work in the social and economic sphere, it would leave the Communists at the starting gate."

I never forgot those words. Indeed, some years later, I repeated them to Archbishop Ricardo Pittini of Santo Domingo. Pittini, an Italian Salesian, passed them on to Pope Pius XII while on a visit to Rome, and in due course the very same thought was expressed by Pius in a major encyclical. So Stanley Smith deserves a footnote in the history of the development of papal social teaching.

The upshot of all this discussion, observation, and reflection, coupled with my talks during previous years with Father Gignac and Father Stringer, was that I was coming to the conclusion that the important thing for a missionary to do was not only to offer the sacraments but to try to help the poor people who were powerless, to save them from their exploiters, to show them how to band together and lift themselves out of their misery. And that, of course, I translated into the process which I had seen work back in my homeland and which was all around me when I was a student at Antigonish and later a priest in my home town, the cooperative movement. Father Coady had always insisted that the priest should be interested in promoting a just economic and social order. If religion and Christianity are to flourish, he would say, we must not overlook the well-being of men. I was thinking more and more about him and about his message of hope, as I made my way slowly back to Canada through India, the Middle East, and Italy, via plane and troop transport. If I was going to continue in the Scarboro Mission Society, I determined, it would not be to repeat elsewhere the procedures that had failed. My missionary vocation, I had become convinced, was to prepare people for the message of Christ by instructing them in the message of Antigonish.

3

DOMINICAN REPUBLIC

Decision to Remain a Missionary

We found it good to be back home in Canada after spending the war years in China, once again among friends, free from aerial bombardment, enjoying three regular meals of nutritious food. Some of my colleagues were down to skin and bone, and several of them would take years to get rid of intestinal parasites and other diseases they had contracted. As for me, while I carried no excess weight, I was in good shape physically. What I did not realize fully for a long time was the depth of the emotional impact. In the First World War they used to talk about shell shock, and the usual term more recently has been combat fatigue. We all had it, each in his own way. In my case, it was aggravated because I was conscious that I had to make a decision that would determine the entire shape of my life.

I had been a priest nine years, seven of them in China. I had had more experience than most priests of my age of the inner workings of the Church, of the jealousies, the ambitions, the manipulations, the legalistic restrictions on dispensing the grace and love of Christ to people who sincerely wanted to live good lives. Both in Canada and in China, I had seen many priests slip into an easy and self-satisfied routine, indifferent to the plights and problems of the people, supportive of the status quo, believing that they were saving the world by distributing the sacraments to people whose need was elementary justice and an opportunity to live their own lives. It was clear in my own mind that I did not want to be that kind of priest. At the same time, I recognized that a priest had many things going for him if he wanted to do something in favor of the poor. I could not forget the comments of my Australian friend, Stanley Smith. He was perfectly right when he said that the Church had a tremendous force of talented people who could make an immense contribution to a better world if they only put their minds to it. I also had the example of Jimmy Tompkins, Moses Coady, Mike Gillis, and the other fine priests associated with them in the cooperative movement right here in Canada. Their work had continued to spread during my absence, in spite of wartime restrictions. It showed that one could be a priest and simultaneously a fighter for social justice. I could see a lot of arguments in favor of being a priest within that kind of framework.

My emotional evolution in China tended on the one side to question the relevance of many of our religious attitudes and values in their traditional expression. The sacraments and other devotional practices all too often degenerated into superstition. But on the other hand, China had deepened and strengthened my basic faith. I find it hard to understand how anyone could live seven years in China, as I did, without a deep sense of religion. Almost by osmosis, some of the attitudes of the Chinese rub off. We called them pagans, yet they were people who lived constantly in the preternatural. Their boats, their rickshaws, their cars are all painted with an eye, a symbol of the beneficent power who protects them from evil. Their home is designed with the same purpose in mind. Everything that happens to them has a significance. Though they are vague in their expression of what is involved, they believe strongly in a supreme being, and it may even be that their vagueness of expression is better than our excessively anthropomorphic formulations of the being and nature of God. Even if I had not previously believed in a life hereafter, I am sure that my exposure to the Chinese would have convinced me of the necessity and reality of life after death, as well as of the ubiquity of providence.

While this mixture of practical and theoretical reasons favored my continuation in the priesthood, the situation at the Scarboro Society made it seem desirable to postpone a firm decision on staying in the Society or leaving it. China was the original Scarboro mission and still its major one, and the entire edifice built up there over many years had been destroyed. Some still hoped that the end of the war would bring a return to normalcy in China, but it was becoming steadily clearer that such a day was away in the distant future, if not a mirage. In addition, many of those who had come home had made up their minds that they were not going back, each for his own reasons, but all basically because they did not feel that the Scarboro authorities back in Canada had given them the support to which they were entitled in their hardships.

After I checked in at Scarboro, I went home to visit my family. I expected, as did my colleagues who were also visiting their families, to learn in due course that another assignment had been arranged. But the months passed, and no news came. After about three months, the same pastor with whom I had worked in my home town of Dominion before leaving for China, invited me to join him once again, and rather than be idle I agreed.

So there I was once more visiting the poor people, checking up on the progress of the housing cooperative, which by now was really thriving and had made a big contribution to the town. Without delay I started the building of another cooperative housing village. During my absence, the cooperative movement had progressed enormously. I found that Father Coady had become a national celebrity, traveling all across Canada to speak to huge audiences, a frequent guest on radio programs.

The impressive thing was that success had not changed him. His speech in public and private was down-to-earth and to the point. And I particularly liked the calm but firm position he took against those of his fellow priests who were apathetic or opposed to his work. Typical of his technique was his reply to one priest who about this time criticized his program. Having rejected as "a monstrous hypocrisy" his opponent's argument that the statement of Jesus that "the poor you have always with you" justified the slum conditions of the proletarian masses in today's cities, he went on:

> I notice that even the clergymen, of all denominations, are interested in having good homes, with bathrooms and good heating systems. They are interested also in social security. Most of them have pensions, and while they are not wealthy, they get enough salary to give them a normal human life. How these men can think that this is necessary for their salvation and not good for the people is more than I can understand. My opinion is that either we clergymen go and live without bathrooms and the other amenities of modern life as so many of the people have to, or if we want these decencies (as we should) then it is our business to do everything we can to get them for the people. We are not fooling the people for a

split second. That may be one of the reasons why we have multi-millions of people in the world today who do not go to church, who can be called only after-Christians or neo-pagans . . . If the people are treated unjustly, then the people will inevitably revolt. . . Therefore, fixing up the economic is a main way and perhaps the only way to ensure law and order and decency and religion in the world. I feel quite certain that the greatest obstacle in the way of doing this is the alliance that has existed for a long time between churchmen and vested interests. Too many of us have been Charlie McCarthys of the financial ventriloquists.

Before long, I made up my mind. I would transfer from the Scarboro Society and join the diocese of Antigonish where I could hope to devote myself to social and economic activities on behalf of the poor while continuing in the priesthood. When I told Father MacRae who was still head of Scarboro, he did everything he could to dissuade me. When I insisted that this was a decision made after mature reflection, he advised me to find out as a first step if Bishop James Morrison of Antigonish would be willing to take me. The bishop had been a friend ever since I was at college. I anticipated no problem with him. However, he cross-examined me as thoroughly as Father MacRae. I told him the truth, namely, that I had not lost interest in mission activities as such, but rather that my idea of what a missionary should be doing was so totally at variance with the views of my colleagues that I saw no way of reconciling the two positions. "I don't know what to decide," he said finally, "because you don't say absolutely that you no longer want to be a missionary. So let me think and pray for a while." After a few weeks I went to see him again. "I have made up my mind," he said. "I think you should

go back to the Scarboro Society and return to the missions."

His answer came as a shock. But it also impressed
me deeply. Obedience was an important thing to me,
and this seemed to be the clear voice of authority. Almost
at the same time something else happened which in a
different way pushed me in the same direction as Bishop
Morrison was pushing me. Father McRae sent me a copy
of a letter he had written to Cardinal Pietro Fumasoni
Biondi, the Prefect of the Congregation of Propaganda,
the Roman congregation to which the Scarboro Society
as a mission group was subject. He told the Cardinal
that I had lost interest in the missions. Now it so happened
that I had tea with the Cardinal in Rome on my way
home from China. I had been given the task of making
a personal report on the situation in China to Pope Pius
XII, and naturally I was first interviewed by the Prefect
of Propaganda before seeing the Pope. During our talk,
I had told the Cardinal that I was thinking of leaving
the Scarboro Society, making it clear that my reason
was not a decline in my interest in the missions but a
belief that I could not carry on an apostolate in favor
of social justice within the framework of any of the existing mission societies. I was very disturbed by the misrep-
resentation of my reasons for wanting to leave, and I
immediately wrote Father McRae telling him to cancel
my application for permission to leave, because I would
not accept it under false pretenses.

At this point, Father Joe MacDonald, the same cousin
whose ordination had so impressed me, and who had
persuaded me to give the seminary a try, once more
played an unanticipated role. During the intervening
years he had won a reputation as an organizer of cooperatives. In 1944 the government of Puerto Rico asked him
to make a survey of the cooperative movement on the
island, because it was in very bad shape. From Puerto

Rico he went to the neighboring Dominican Republic to visit the Scarboro priests who were working there, several of whom he knew, arriving by coincidence on the day a disastrous earthquake struck the island, August 4, 1945. One of the people he met was the head of the church in the Dominican Republic, Archbishop Ricardo Pittini, an Italian Salesian whose concern for the poor was in the tradition of Don Bosco, who had founded the Salesians. The Archbishop had long been badgering the Scarboro priests to do something for the forgotten people of the Dominican Republic, and he repeated his thoughts to Joe MacDonald. So when Joe came back, he visited me. He had heard of my plans to join the Antigonish diocese. "Don't leave Scarboro," he told me. "Go down to Santo Domingo. This is the challenge you have been looking for all your life." And Father Alphonsus Chafe, the Scarboro superior in the Dominican Republic, wrote me in the same vein. "Here are three million people waiting for you, and you will have all the scope you want, because the Archbishop is the one who is pushing it."

I didn't know a word of Spanish when I arrived in the Dominican Republic in 1946. And at that time the Society had no formal arrangements for teaching it. I was sent first to live with another Scarboro priest at a place called Consuelo, where there was a sugar factory and some people spoke English. But my colleague was busy and he couldn't find a Spanish teacher for me. As a result I wasted two months. Then another colleague, Father Pat Moore, went on vacation. He had a small parish in the remote countryside, at a village called Boyá. There was no access road, and the only way in was on horseback. I agreed to replace him during his absence, which was to be for not more than two months but which ended up as two years. It was an extraordinary experience to be marooned in a place so primitive, but it was ultimately most fruitful, because it gave me not only the language of the people but a unique close-up view of their culture, values, and philosphy. Few priests ever have such an experience. They live in a town and visit these remote villages from time to time, staying perhaps one day, seldom more than three or four. And during these visits, everyone is on his best behavior and the priest remains an outsider.

Boyá was just a plaza, about two hundred yards long, and a hundred wide. .It was very old, with the houses all around a circle, the way the Indians used to live. It was, in fact, the only remaining relic in the Dominican Republic of the aboriginal Arawak Indians. It's where the great Enrequillo, the last Indian to stand up against the Spaniards, was buried. It is where they later built a national shrine to holy water, La Virgen del Aqua Santa. Wherever that came from God knows, some superstition. Each day the people go out into the countryside three or four or five miles, where they have their small farms, or *canucos* as they call them. Many of them have a mule, a donkey or a little horse, and some hens and pigs. Occasionally you might see a duck but not too often. No sheep or goats, although in other places you find goats. An occasional person would have a cow, but for all practical purposes, there was no milk in their lives. Neither did they eat meals in our sense, no sitting down together at a fixed time. When a child got hungry, his mother would give him a piece of corn to chew on or a piece of yucca or a mango. A meal of some kind would be cooked, but there was no question of sitting down to a table. Most of them couldn't afford to eat rice. They had to sell it to buy clothing and medicine. They eat yucca and other starchy vegetables. The only meat was when someone killed a pig. Then it all had to be eaten up, because there was no way to keep it.

Boyá consisted of forty or fifty families, no road, no

post office, no electricity, not even running water. It did have a one-teacher government school consisting of the first three grades. But even that was recent and practically none of the adults could read or write. The rectory was a little shack with clapboard walls and a palm-thatch roof. The chapel was of similar construction, with a mud floor. An old lady who lived next door prepared my food and brought it to me. She did my laundry and kept the church linens in order, and the combined food and service cost me a dollar a day.

My teacher was a ten-year-old boy who had just completed the third grade in school. He was an altar boy, and he was one of the few people in the village able to read and write. So for the best part of each day, I would sit in an old wicker chair in my home, with the door wide open to catch the breeze. His friends would come along with my teacher, and everyone would join in the fun. I would study my grammar and check words in the dictionary, forming sentences and getting the correct sounds from the children. At first they were scared of me, never having had any dealings with an outsider. But after about six months of constant living together, the barriers started to come down. To the casual observer, the life of the poor man is very simple, with everything in his little shack exposed literally to the public gaze. But actually he constructs elaborate defenses, anxious most of all to be invisible and unnoticed because he does not know how to function in that other world of the rich and powerful. It was during those two years in Boyá that I became part of that secret world of the poor, a vision and an opportunity vouchsafed to few and of priceless worth.

My parish stretched for miles in all directions with a total population of twenty thousand or more. After about six months, when I had acquired some familiarity with the language, I began to visit the other villages to say Mass, baptize the infants, and see that everything was going along satisfactorily. The basis of the economy was mixed farming conducted at a very primitive level. The land was poor to start, and the people had no idea of how to use it. None of them had titles to the land. Technically, it all belonged to the Church, as is common in many parts of Latin America, under grants from the Spanish crown going back to the sixteenth century. But the Church collected no rents, nor did it exercise any rights of ownership. A man just picked an idle piece of land, the size depending on his own willingness to work and the number of helpers in his family, then slashed and burned it to clear the ground, and set corn, rice, or yucca. Those who were better off had a wooden plow and oxen, or at least rented them to prepare the land. But most of them just put holes in the ground with a stick. In a few years, when the fertility of the virgin soil had been depleted, a man moved on to a new location. In some areas, there was better land in private ownership, and there the peasant usually sharecropped, giving the owner half the produce.

Most of what the peasant family consumes is produced on this plot of land, but he has to buy salt, medicines, and usually a few groceries, and that is where the *patrón* system comes into play, a system which operates at all levels in Latin America. The *patrón* is the person above you with some access to wealth and power to whom you turn whenever life becomes too complicated for you to handle it by yourself. With the peasant, the usual *patrón* is the merchant, of whom we had three in Boyá. Each merchant is decision maker, general confessor, and fixer for his clients. In return, he owns them body and soul. He gives them credit for seeds, and for whatever they buy in his general store while the crop is growing. At harvest time, they bring the crop to him or he goes out with his mules to collect it, paying whatever price he determines. If a member of the family is seriously ill, the *patrón*'s horse carries him to a hospital. The merchant lives well. The peasant knows that he is being bled, but he is philosophical about it. He lacks options. "I would get twice the price if I sold the rice myself," he will say. "But what can I do? The *patrón* is my protection, my womb. He saved my mother's life three years ago. Without him I would be lost." And most of these merchants are in fact not monsters. Rather they are small parasites carrying much bigger ones on their own backs in a man-destroying parasitic system.

The priest also is trapped in his own way in the system. After I learned the language, I found I had relatively little to do. There were eight or nine sectors in the parish, each with a village where the priest went to celebrate Mass and administer the sacraments. But I soon learned that each of these wanted the priest to come only once or at most twice a year. When they had a fiesta to celebrate the feast day of their patron saint, it was essential to have the priest. They prepared for the event for weeks, dressing up in their best clothes. But they couldn't afford that too often. And they soon let me understand that a little religion went a long way with them. Sure they wanted me back, but not too soon.

The issue wasn't primarily what the priest himself got out of it, but rather the disturbance of the rhythm of village life by his too frequent presence. As far as the priest was concerned, he got all he was going to get if he came only once a year. The collection in the church during service was minimal. His fees came mostly from baptisms, each of which brought a dollar and a half, and from the so-called responses. The responses were prayers for the dead, and that was what people mostly valued, although largely for superstitious reasons. The prayer in question was the *Libera* from the burial service, and people believed that it had special efficacy for a dead person if the priest read it. The fee was 25 cents for reciting it and 50 cents for singing it. Any time you visited a village, you would get ten or twenty dollars for responses in favor of persons who had died since your previous visit.

The big time for the responses was on All Souls Day or on the day closest to it that the priest happened to be in a particular place. He would have to go to the cemetery and go from grave to grave, sprinkling holy water and singing the *Libera* until his throat was sore and he lost his voice. I remember once in a place called Los Alcarrizos, I had been doing this all evening, with hundred of candles burning all through the cemetery, and at two in the morning I still had people waiting for me. Then an old lady came up and asked me to go to a grave a hundred yards away. I was dogtired and I said, jokingly, "I'm getting old and I have a wooden leg. Do you think the blessing will carry if I do it from here?" A little girl who was with the woman put her hand down and felt my two legs under my cassock. "They are not wooden," she said indignantly. We all laughed, and I had to carry my weary body to perform the ceremony in the proper way. Another time I remember making a bet with two other priests to see which of us would sing the most *Liberas* on a particular All Souls Day. Each of us covered several cemeteries, and the total take for the day between us was about $500, of which I myself contributed more than $200. But that was the major income of the priest for the whole year, that and the baptisms which could come to fifty or more when you visited a village after a long absence.

Starting a Credit Union

With time on my hands in between my visits to the outlying villages, I naturally began to think of my purpose in coming to the Dominican Republic, and I decided I would try to start a credit union. The first problem was to get the men together, because only one or two of them came to Mass on a regular Sunday, apart from their annual fiesta. So I sent word to them through the women that I wanted them to come for a meeting on a certain afternoon, and I also passed the word to some other villages which were not too far away. About fifty showed up on the appointed day. I talked to them for about two hours, trying to get across the basic concept of the credit union as an association of the people of the community, each of whom would undertake to make a regular payment of a small amount of money, the capital thus accumulated to be available for lending to the members at minimum rates of interest. I pointed out that this was the first step toward freeing the poor from their greatest enemy, the moneylender who keeps them in perpetual debt by charging them interest rates of 20 percent or more. All of them had experience of the loan shark and they agreed in principle that life would be paradise if they could get him permanently off their backs. But life has an inevitability for the peasant. It was always like that, and it would always be like that. He looks with suspicion at a new idea, turning it over at a respectable distance. You can show him that it works, but it is not easy to convince him that it will work for him. That is his lifelong experience, as it was that of his father and his grandfather before him.

After a long and inconclusive exchange, we agreed to meet again a week later. There were two or three new faces, but nine or ten of the original group were missing. And so it went on each week for five or six weeks. By then we had thinned out to seven or eight, and I decided they would serve as a nucleus. So I told them I recognized that they were really interested and I said we were ready to begin. The only way they could prove the thing to themselves was by saving for two or three years in order not only to accumulate capital but to learn by regular study how to use it fruitfully to lift themselves out of their misery. I was forced to become the treasurer, because they wouldn't trust any of themselves, and there was no bank nearer than the capital eighty miles away, a whole day's journey at that time. The weekly quota was five cents, which was all most could afford, although a few agreed to pay a dime. Our entire accounting system was a single notebook, in which I entered each name, with the date and amount of each payment. Gradually we worked up a little enthusiasm. There were two brothers in the village who were solid citizens, more intelligent than the others, and they could read and write a little. They would go around trying to persuade the others to join, and they had some success. Several people wanted to send in their money without coming to the weekly meetings, but I refused to take them, explaining that the primary benefit of the credit union is the education in handling money. The group would have no future unless the members learned how to run it properly.

I kept pounding the principles into them. I had a few pamphlets in English, nothing at that time in Spanish, and I typed up and mimeographed some sheets to serve as class texts. But the almost total illiteracy, combined with the very low level of culture, was too much for me. The people in this part of the island were mostly descendants of African slaves, and they had lived for hundreds of years in isolation and deprivation. Their ancestors had been stripped of their traditional culture in the process of enslavement and transfer to America, and the subsequent neglect of their masters and of the government had left them at a cultural and intellectual level little above their animals. Try as they might, they could learn little and understand less. It was a situation radically different from that back in Nova Scotia or from that in the countries of Europe and North America where the credit union had previously been introduced. There, the people were poor and often with little formal education. But they did have a cultural accumulation of the natural virtues of self-respect, thrift, honesty, and work. If they did not always practice these virtues, at least they knew what they were. And thus gradually my experience brought me to recognize the absolute need of a certain minimum human level of development as a precondition for the establishment of credit unions or cooperatives.

In subsequent years, I have seen all kinds of efforts, many of them highly subsidized, go down to destruction because of the violation of this rule. The paternalistic temptation becomes very great in these circumstances. It is easy to set up the formal structures and have a Peace Corps volunteer or some other social worker assume total responsibility for policy and supervision. But it is a house built on sand so long as the members are not themselves responsible for every decision, for every loan, for the accuracy of every audit of the books. To be able to borrow a few dollars at low interest is a benefit for the peasant. But what really changes him is to acquire a mentality which enables and authorizes him to manage a small business, such as the typical credit union is. This mentality feeds back into his handling of his own affairs and is quickly expressed in better habits of work, more care for his tools and animals, planning of expeditures to permit capital improvements in his home and on his farm, in a word, the take-off to prosperity.

Try as I might, I was unable to carry the Boyá credit union beyond the formative stage. Once a group is formed, each man commits himself to make a weekly payment, and after about a year, some would have perhaps five dollars in their account. Then a man would be faced with a real emergency and would ask for his money, as he was entitled to do at any time. This created a problem for me. Because the group was not sufficiently developed and trained, we were not yet legally constituted as a credit union, and in consequence we were not authorized to make loans. At the same time I knew that if I just gave the man back his money, that was the end of him, and soon it would be the end of the group. I decided I would myself set up and control the books for emergency loans backed by the savings of the borrower. Instead of giving the man his own five dollars, I would lend him five under a commitment to repay at a stipulated rate. It was a good try, but it didn't work. Once the man got his money, he went away and we never saw him again. He felt he had lost face by taking his money out. And as one after another did the same thing, we ran right into the ground. Two or three members wanted to continue, and I made a second try. But it ended up like the first. The human basis just didn't exist and could not be improvised. It was a harsh lesson but an important one.

My experience in several neighboring towns and villages was substantially the same. Even before I had come to the Dominican Republic, two of my Scarboro colleagues, Father Chafe, the superior, and Father Jimmy Walsh, had tried to set up credit unions, although neither of them had previous experience of the system and thought that the main idea was simply to accumulate enough capital to be able to provide low-interest loans. When I finally gave up in Boyá after nearly two years and moved to the capital city, Father Walsh was in Bayaguana a short distance down the road and had been working with a savings group there for nearly a year. I got one going in Monte Plata also, and I would also visit Bayaguana regularly and try to get a proper study program going. But we never got very far. Things went well only as long as the priest retained responsibility for everything. He was the only person to whom the people would entrust their money, and he had to keep the books and make all the decisions. It was only a parody of the real thing, because the moment an interested priest left the town, the entire edifice collapsed.

In Monte Plata I was also learning other disconcerting things about the way business is conducted in Latin America. At the beginning I could get only the women to take an interest, and one of the first men to join was a dentist. He had been educated abroad and was a man of standing in the town. His enthusiasm for the credit union idea was boundless and he helped me greatly to spread the interest, even enlisting three or four other men. Then I had to leave for a time, and the members—still almost all women—decided to put the dentist in charge during my absence. When I came back, the credit union had folded up. It took me some time to reconstruct the events. My friend had learned all too well that the essence of the program was instruction of the members. So instead of continuing with the kind of informal classes which I had run, he tried to turn the meetings into a school of the kind he knew, a school where an all-knowing teacher pounded knowledge into the heads of ignorant and unwilling pupils. The people were fairly ignorant, but were by no means unwilling. So they resented the new relationship, however well intentioned, and they simply stopped coming.

That was but one of several embarrassments. Another man, a petty town official, had also distinguished himself as a promoter of the credit union. He wanted to learn everything, and he excelled in recruiting members. It took me six months to discover who he was. He was the biggest loan shark in town. On weekends he rode out on his horse into the country to make new loans and collect on the old ones. The credit union was the best thing that ever happened for him, because he was able to borrow from it at low interest and lend in the country at usurious rates. So, of course, I had to get rid of him and create an enemy.

Then there was the sacristan of one of my fellow pastors, an elderly lady who lived in the church, at Mass every morning in the week and a regular receiver of the sacraments. She was an outstanding member of the credit union, borrowing substantial sums and always prompt with her payments. Everyone in town knew what she was doing with the money, everyone but the pastor. Then one day it came to light that she was the owner of the town's biggest house of prostitution, and that she was using the money to build an annex and expand her business. She was indignant when she was told she could not continue her membership, insisting that her business was perfectly legal, as it was in the Dominican Republic. The distinction between legal and ethical seemed to escape her.

There were other things I learned the hard way too. For example, you can't mix the town folk and those from the country, at least at the start. At a Sunday Mass in a small town, most of the men present are from the surrounding countryside. If you persuade them to stay over after Mass for a meeting to dicuss a credit union, none of the men from the town will participate. They look down on the *campesinos* and would consider it a loss of face to be mixed up with them. Similarly, if you start with the women, as I did at Monte Plata, you can't get the men to join. That goes for everything. In most parts of Latin America, men don't go to Mass on Sunday because that is a business for women. I tested that out practically once by setting up a Mass for men only. I had the greatest trouble in keeping the women out and made several enemies. But I persevered and it worked. Soon the men were coming in large numbers to *their* Mass. Later on, in the case of the credit union or the cooperative, when the men have made it their own, they can be persuaded to allow women to join them. But the pecking order is well established and you can bypass it only at your own risk.

Needless to say, these negative experiences at Boyá, Monte Plata, and the other neighboring localities caused me to question my basic assumptions. All I really had to go on was that the cooperative system had worked very well in the Maritime Provinces of Canada when presented as a self-help and community-building program within the spirit developed at Antigonish. Here I was attempting the same approach and getting nowhere. Could it be that the system was not suited to the conditions of the Dominican Republic and other parts of Latin America? One day I expressed my concern to Hans Schnaubel. Hans was a Dominican of German parentage, a man of about sixty with some knowledge of the world. He had formerly owned and operated a small rice-processing factory and sawmill in Boyá, and he was the owner of the small house in which I lived there. "Don't give up so easily," he urged me. "In this area, unfortunately, you lack the human base on which to build. But you were unlucky to start here. Now, over in the Cibao things are totally different. There you have people with a stable family tradition, a sense of honor, self-respect. Things work differently there."

In due course I was to confirm the accuracy of his evaluation. But first I had to go back to our central house in Santo Domingo, the capital, or Ciudad Trujillo as the dictator of that time had renamed it in his own honor. They needed a procurator or business manager, the same job I had performed in China. The job was a part-time one, and Father Chafe's idea was that it would leave me free time to experiment with the cooperative movement in the city. He himself had already been talking to postal workers about a credit union, and we went ahead from where he was. In a city, where people have regular wages, it is not so hard to build up a substantial capital. But there also, in our anxiety for some results to show, we tried to go too fast. In one center, we had accumulated $5,000 and we had to give it all back and close out the group. We just couldn't get eleven people to constitute the directorate and the various committees without which a credit union cannot function. The men wouldn't come, and the women didn't know how to read or write, and they were having so many children that you had no continuity.

All this time, I had not forgotten Hans Schnaubel's comments about the Cibao. This region lies right across the island from the capital near the north shore, but it was relatively easy to reach because the highway to Santiago, the second city of the Dominican Republic, had cut the distance to three hours by car. And since I took over the procurator's job, I had become the possessor of a second-hand automobile. So I began to explore the Cibao, where a missionary society from French-speaking Canada was in charge of fourteen or fifteen parishes. The first man to welcome me was Father Carlos Guillot, a big, tough, husky Quebecker, built like a football player. He looked for all the world like Jack Dempsey, only that he was a little shorter. He was a tremendous worker, rough in his ways, but with a heart of gold. The people called him Father Dynamite. I have seldom met a foreigner who could speak such excellent Spanish.

I was amazed to discover that all these Quebeckers knew absolutely nothing about the credit union movement, although the first credit unions in the New World had been set up in Quebec by Alphonse Desjardins at the beginning of the century, and the movement had grown to the point where the credit union bank was one of the biggest banks in North America. Of course, they had all gone off to seminaries when they were ten years old and had been isolated from that time onward, so they knew nothing about their own province. But when I told them what Alphonse Desjardins had done and what I was trying to do, they thought the idea was marvelous and offered to do all they could to help me. And down through the years they have been faithful to that undertaking. Indeed, I have gotten far more support from them than from most of my own colleagues of the Scarboro Society.

I soon confirmed for myself that Hans Schnaubel had been right about the people of the Cibao. I think of a village called Guayabal, an hour or two from Santiago. Never in my life did I find such fine people anywhere in the world. They were very poor. They owned their own land, but they have huge families of ten or fifteen, and over the generations the farms had been divided up among the children until some of them are down to a patch the size of a city building lot. But the moral caliber of these people was magnificent. Once they put their mind to something, they stayed with it through thick and thin.

In addition to the priests, I quickly found lay helpers among all levels of society. One of the first was Saulio Saleta, a small merchant of Santiago. He was a man of extraordinary social sensitivity, always concerned for the poor and opposed to injustice of every kind. Inevitably, he suffered much for his open expression of his views in Trujillo's dictatorship, but fortunately for him Trujillo always avoided applying in the Cibao the brutal terror tactics with which he oppressed the people in the rest of the country. Nobody ever knew just why, but apparently he suspected that if he pushed these independent-minded people too hard, he might be the loser. In any case, Saleta survived and is today a moderately successful businessman, but still an ardent supporter of cooperatives and of everything calculated to lessen the social inequities under which the great majority of Dominicans still suffer. In those early days, Saleta put himself and his car at my disposal, devoting all his spare time, and even time he should have been working, to going around the villages and spreading the good news of the credit union and cooperative movement.

Then there was Emilio Batista, a thirty-two-year-old *campesino* from La Torre. I had gone there at the invitation of the pastor, a Jesuit named Gerardo Vázquez. The credit union was a success at La Torre from the start. In two months, 400 men were inscribed on the rolls and savings had grown to a thousand dollars. The enthusiasm was enormous, and I have always given the credit to Emilio. His goodness impressed me from our first meeting. He was typical of the region in many ways, extremely poor, barely able to read or write having completed three grades at school, married four years and already father of four children. But what was special about him was his humility and his sincerity. All that man needed, I told myself, was a chance to exercise his natural qualities of leadership. And in due course the opportunity developed to prove that my hunch was correct.

To explain how this happened, I must digress for a moment. I was still living in our central house, taking care of the finances and helping with various efforts to start credit unions in the neighborhood of the capital, while taking two or three days for a visit to the Cibao as often as I could spare the time. The rapid expansion of the movement, particularly in the Cibao, was beginning to attract attention, and various reports about us had been published in the newspapers. Now this society of the Dominican Republic under the dictatorship of the Benefactor, Generalissimo Rafael Leónidas Trujillo

Molino, Father of the Fatherland and Founder of the New Era, was something unique. When the United States military occupation, which had grown out of an arrange-ment made in 1905 for United States administration of the customs, came to an end in 1924, Trujillo had worked himself up in their puppet regime to the position of chief of police. By 1930 he had risen to the top as undisputed dictator, and there he stayed until assassinated in 1961.

The first and only rule of conduct in the Dominican Republic was that nobody did anything without Trujillo's approval. To cross him even in a detail was to invite physical assault. Joaquín Balaguer, who has been presi-dent of the Dominican Republic since 1966, once appeared in public when he was vice-president with a black eye. Trujillo had beaten him up. He was a madman when he was drunk. The classic story about him involves the killing of an Episcopalian missionary from the United States in 1934. The latter used to write to his brother back home about the violations of human rights under Trujillo, and some of the stories got into the New York newspapers. Trujillo, who spent millions on buying him-self a favorable press in the United States, said this had to stop. The missionary was warned, but he ignored the warnings. Then one night he was summoned to attend to a dying communicant. When he arrived, he was ushered into the presence of Trujillo and seven or eight of his aides. "I warned you," he said, signaling to the others to grab the man and throw him on the floor, then started to jump on him until his face and head were smashed beyond recognition. "Finish him off," he told the others, stalking from the room. That was reputedly the one time he participated personally in a killing. But he had the process well organized. Over the years he probably had a hundred thousand people killed. In one day alone his men slaughtered thirty thousand Haitians in cold blood.

After I had been working with the Cibao people for about a year, I got a call one day from a government official who told me that Manuel Peña Batlle wanted to see me. Of Basque extraction and a lawyer, Peña Batlle was the second most powerful man in the Dominican Republic at that time, and although he was totally loyal to Trujillo, he had the reputation of being a fair man who always wanted to do the right thing, a reputation to which he lived up fully in my subsequent dealings with him. As any call from a government official could mean trouble, I went along with a certain amount of trepidation. To my relief, I found he had been favorably impressed with the reports about the cooperative movement and wanted to hear more about it. As he listened, he grew enthusiastic. "This is the greatest thing that ever came to our country," he said finally. "What do you need to keep it going?"

I had my answer well prepared, because that was the question I had been pondering for months as I drove back and forth to the Cibao. "What we need now are leaders," I told him. "I have set up what can be called pilot projects and I have demonstrated that the Antigonish system can work in the Dominican Republic. But I am already beyond the limit of what one person can do. I spend half a day with the farmers in San José de las Matas or La Torre or Moca, and then I don't see them again for a month. The whole secret of this movement is the self-education, the continual discussion by people of their own problems leading to agreement on total community effort to resolve them. This is quite different from somebody coming in from the outside to give them a set of rules. It is their own self-discovery as people, and the one who can best help them is one of themselves who has the necessary training. That is what I see as the next step, a center where I can bring the natural leaders for short courses. Two or three weeks is enough

to start. Then bring another group, and another. After
a year or so, I get the original group back for a second
course and later for a third, and so on. That is how the
Antigonish people do it, and it works.''

We agreed that I needed a building that would have
dormitory and classroom space for fifteen or twenty
people. Peña Batlle was independently wealthy, and he
took me to see several pieces of land he owned, but
I hesitated to accept any of them because of the difficulty
of getting water, electricity, or an access road. In addition, Archbishop Pittini had warned me never to accept
a gift of land from anyone. ''It can be a nominal price,''
he said, ''but it must always be a deed of sale, because
nobody in this country has a clear title to anything, and
you'll be in trouble when the donor dies or when you
want to sell.'' It was good advice, and it is valid in most
parts of Latin America. So while I was hesitating, Peña
Batlle told Trujillo, with whom he was in daily contact,
what he was planning. And Trujillo, as usual, wanted
to get into the action. ''I'll give him whatever money
he needs,'' he told Peña Batlle. In due course I received
a check for $19,000, with which in August 1951 I bought
land and started the building. That was characteristic
of Trujillo. I'd be needing more, but he liked to keep
people on a string. I would have to come back.

I hired a carpenter, a mason, and about thirty workmen.
It was simple construction and I had learned something
about building when I was involved in the cooperative
housing programs back in Canada. By the time the money
ran out, we were about three-quarters completed. I went
back to Peña Batlle. ''I can't talk to Trujillo now,'' he
told me, ''nobody can talk to him. He's a raving madman.
You'll just have to wait.'' What had happened was that
one of Trujillo's brothers had been discovered attempting
to pass $5 or $10 million of counterfeit bills, and Trujillo
was planning to have him assassinated. The coun-

try was in chaos and everyone expected a revolution. His mother finally persuaded Trujillo to exile the offending brother to Spain, but he continued to rage and to work off his fury on everyone who came near him. "Give him three months or six months to cool down," the nuncio advised me. "That's the only way to live with him."

I was frustrated, but all I could do was let my workers go, and wait for fair weather. Then one day I went to visit a member of the Vicini family, a lawyer. His name was Cabral—his mother was a Vicini. The Vicinis are of Italian extraction. They have been several generations in the Dominican Republic, and they own three sugar plantations. I told him the story of my activities, and he was amazed. "I am a Catholic," he said, "as my family has been from away back, and this is the first Christian thing I ever heard that anyone in the Church was doing. How much do you need?" I told him I needed $10,000 to put a roof on my building. "Come back tomorrow morning," he said. Here was a man I had met for the first time in my life. I could not believe he was serious. But I had nothing to lose, so I came back in the morning and he handed me a check for $10,000. By the time the roof was on, Trujillo had calmed down a bit, and Peña Batlle gave me $5,000 for furniture and equipment. There still was the problem of running costs, because when I got into action with a constant succession of courses and a staff of a dozen people, the budget came to $40,000 or $50,000 a year. Through Peña Batlle and Manuel Moya, who was another of Trujillo's top aides, I received a regular grant of $10,000 a year. The rest I had to raise myself through friends in the United States and Canada.

The first course ran two weeks, and it opened on March 1, 1952, with seventeen students, ten from the Cibao. We were starting without any previous experience to guide us, and inevitably we made mistakes. One of the first things I learned was not to take students under twenty years of age or over forty. The best age seemed to be twenty-five to thirty-five. As a further indication of the quality of the Cibao men, they took the first three places in the examinations, although they had been studying for a much shorter time than those from the south.

Emilio Batista, My First Assistant

Emilio Batista from La Torre was a student in the first course I gave at the new center, and he also became my first assistant. I hired him part-time, because that was all that I could afford, and because he still had to care for his little farm. Then a short time later, Fernando Chávez, who was in charge of cooperative activities for the Pan American Union in Washington, offered the Dominican Republic three scholarships for a six-month training course in Puerto Rico. Our movement was the only one in the Dominican Republic, but the whole country was run on the basis of graft and politics, and the government decided to send three of its own people who could have a good time at public expense. After a big tussle, I managed to get one scholarship, and I sent Emilio. It was a tough struggle for him, because the other twenty-five or thirty people from eight or ten neighboring countries had far more academic training. But he was dogged, and by the end the professors agreed unanimously that he was the star pupil in the course.

Before long, I was able to employ him full-time, and it was the best decision I ever made. This man has a magic with *campesinos*. He doesn't articulate well, his language is not always grammatical. But he speaks their language, he is their man. His entire life is of one piece, a man of integrity, of dignity, of honor. One of the most touching moments of my life was one day when I called at his home unexpectedly. It was a tiny place, little more than a shack, with clapboard walls, cradled in the slope of a hill. Three or four little children were playing in the dirt outside. "Where is your father?" I asked. One got up and ran into the house without answering, and as I followed I was met at the door by Emilio, who was weeping. I knew something was terribly wrong, because he is normally reserved and self-controlled. Then his wife came and she too was weeping. But they couldn't express their grief in words. They just took me inside. In these little houses, the beds are adjoining, so that sometimes you can't even walk between them. There were three beds in the room, and lying on one of them was a baby that had died an hour or two before. They had had no money to get a doctor. They had no money to pay for his burial. They were simply two human beings overwhelmed by circumstances which they lacked the means to deal with. But what I saw at that moment was their great love for their baby and for each other. I saw two of the greatest human beings in the world.

I know there are many Emilio Batistas in the Dominican Republic, in Costa Rica, and in Panama, and in every valley of the Andes, and all around the world, natural leaders who need only half a chance to make the world better for themselves and for their neighbors. How long more must we wait before giving all of them their chance?

The other side of the coin is that all the foreign aid and technical assistance in the world won't make a dent as long as we try to bypass the Emilio Batistas. The peasant doesn't trust any outsider, and he is perfectly right. That is the principle of survival that has been bred into him over a hundred generations. Anytime he gets mixed up with that other world of power and technology. he always comes out with the short straw.

I once used Emilio to demonstrate that principle. It was in the days when United States aid was known as Point Four, and a tobacco expert had come down to show the people in the Cibao how to improve the quality of their product. He was a really fine person, already elderly but very dedicated. Most of his working life had been spent in Turkey and other parts of the Middle East, and he had come back from retirement to do this job. With him was a team of Americans and Dominicans, and they had spent a pile of money with nothing to show for it. One day he appealed to me for help. "Where in this area are the most enterprising farmers?" he asked. "I can show them how to double their profits by using disinfectants and fertilizers and by caring properly for the plants." I talked to Emilio and we got together about five hundred men from a number of cooperatives. They listened, they asked questions, they measured out the fungicides and noted the symptoms. The Point Four people were delighted. It was their finest presentation.

A few days later I met my friend. "That was a real breakthrough," he said, "and I have to thank you for it." I said nothing, and he understood my silence. "Let me have it," he said. "Your boys did their job perfectly," I told him, "but you still haven't got to first base. These men live from hand to mouth. They get a hundred dollars or at most two hundred from their tobacco crop the way they grow it. To lose one crop would be the end. They need that money to repay their loans, to buy clothing, medicine, salt, sugar, and so on. They know you can do it the other way, the better way, but they are not convinced that they can, and they simply cannot afford the risk. They would be wiped out."

How could the vicious circle be broken? Only by having some of the farmers themselves demonstrate the benefits of the new techniques, guaranteeing them against loss in the process. So I said I had three employees in the group, and that I would guarantee to them the same payment for the next crop as they got for last year's, plus any additional money it might bring when sold. Emilio and the two others agreed. In one year they doubled their income and the following year it was even higher. Then the neighbors began to take notice, and within five years hundreds of others were imitating them. Now, twenty years later, the nature of the tobacco industry of this region has changed totally through the production of a better quality product.

Another of my early employees was José Bisonó. His background was also in farming, although when I met him he lived in the town of San José de las Matas, where he had been running a small business until he fell sick and had to give it up. While he was convalescing, I started a credit union in the town and he came to a couple of the talks. He was a bookkeeper with a high-school education, not a *campesino* like Emilio. He didn't have quite the same magic with the people, but he made up for it by his honesty and dedication. There are good people everywhere if you know how to find them.

By now I was mostly involved myself with running the training center and raising money to keep it going. Each year we had ten to fifteen 3-week courses, with about twenty students in each, so that within a few years we had one or two leaders in every village who had enough knowledge and self-assurance to keep the credit unions going, and to encourage the people to move on to forming a consumer cooperative and a marketing cooperative, for which the credit union was just the forerunner. When a village has a marketing cooperative, the members are able to get the market price for what they have to sell, eliminating the middlemen. Similarly, the consumer cooperative means he can get his sugar, salt, seeds, and other essentials at a fair price, breaking the stranglehold of the merchants. Naturally, at this point you run up against vested interests, and that is precisely what happened to us. The first danger sign came when I was talking to the Chamber of Commerce of the city of La Vega, a small town of some 25,000 people at that time.

They had asked me to explain the cooperative movement to them, and I was glad to comply. Then the questions came from the merchants and professional people in the audience. "If this works," one of them said, "you are going to take over the country." I assured them that even in the countries with the most highly developed cooperative movement this had nowhere happened. But they saw the danger. What undoubtedly disturbed them most was the new spirit developing among the *campesinos*. Whenever I called for a meeting in La Vega or any other large town, five or six hundred men would appear as if by magic from the surrounding villages to spend an entire day discussing their problems. It was a real revolution, because up to that time the poor man, when he had a problem, went hat in hand to the merchant, the lawyer, or the politician, accepting the decision of the *patrón* no matter how biased by self-interest.

It had taken eight or nine years to reach this point of challenge. I had come to the Dominican Republic in 1946 and the Chamber of Commerce meeting in La Vega occurred about 1955. We really had come along fast. We had a network of credit unions throughout the island and a good sprinkling of marketing and consumer cooperatives, many of them owning buildings worth thousands of dollars. We had obtained a cooperative law to enable us to incorporate and give legal personality to the various groups. We had set up a federation and each year brought a hundred or more delegates to a national reunion. But, as I was discovering, we were not over the hump. On the contrary, we were facing the dilemma which no cooperative movement in any poor country has yet resolved. How do you break out of unjust structures, when the structures have a monopoly of political and police power, while all you have on your side is right? That is the question the twentieth century has not yet answered.

It is interesting, for example, throughout Latin America today to see the difference in the emphasis which big business, and the governments and international organizations which reflect the views of big business, place on credit unions on the one hand, and on marketing and consumer cooperatives on the other. Everybody is in favor of credit unions. United States foreign aid is channeled generously in their direction for the training of leaders and the expansion of their lending operations. The reason is that they are relatively harmless. They neither help nor hurt very much by themselves, while to support them creates an impression of concern for the small man. Even bankers welcome them, because they get money out of mattresses and into banks. But the marketing and consumer cooperatives challenge the system. They immediately destroy the monopoly of decision-making and price-fixing hitherto enjoyed by the business community. When the *campesinos* realize the change the cooperatives are effecting in their favor, they quickly turn to an examination of the other factors that are holding them back. Very soon the struggle for land reform intensifies. That is where the battle must ultimately be joined. Until he owns his land, the *campesino* is at the mercy of the man who owns it. He can begin his liberation through credit unions and cooperatives, but his efforts at building cooperatives will always ultimately be thwarted until he builds his own power base through land ownership. And if those in possession continue to use their power to prevent this peaceful development, then the only outlet left is violence leading to socialism or communism, the direction in which Latin America is actually moving.

To get back to the Dominican Republic, after the Chamber of Commerce meeting at La Vega, the merchants passed the word to merchants around the island and to their political cronies, and soon the harassment of cooperative leaders became evident. I was tailed by spies wherever I went, and I knew reports were being made to the authorities. Trujillo feared nothing so much as the development of any group activity which he did not totally control. At the same time, I felt fairly secure as long as Dr. Peña Batlle was protecting me from his position at the dictator's side. I kept him fully informed of everything and he always backed me a hundred percent. The situation was such, nevertheless, that one always ran the risk of clashing with somebody in authority, and the personalist type of government meant that the outcome was always arbitrary, one way or the other.

There was, for example, the problem of the insurance with the Credit Union National Association of the United States (CUNA). This organization, established in 1935, groups the more than twenty million credit union members in the United States and it has links with many more millions in other countries. One of the benefits of membership is the opportunity to participate in an insurance program which pays $10,000 to the estate of a member who dies. Another CUNA insurance not only cancels a member's outstanding loans from his credit union, but also pays his estate double his accumulated savings. The premiums are low and are paid from the profits of each participating credit union, so that the individual member sees himself as getting something for nothing.

The advantage of the CUNA insurance was tremendous not only in itself but as a measure of the progress of the credit union movement in the Dominican Republic. To qualify, a federation had to measure up to strict rules of accounting and procedures. We passed the tests successfully, then discovered a major snag. To obtain the funds to pay the premium in the United States we would have to register under the insurance laws and deposit with the government something like half a million dollars as a guarantee of our financial stability. With Peña Batlle's approval, I shortcircuited this process by having the Scarboro Society pay the premiums from funds which other wise they would have remitted for the maintenance of the priests, and I reimbursed Scarboro in the Dominican Republic.

The very first claim, however, created an unanticipated problem. A man in the village of La Torre was killed one night in his home while he was leading his family in the rosary. A neighbor, who had been refused a loan by the credit committee of the village credit union, burst in and stuck a knife in him. Now one of Trujillo's many quirks was an insistence that the people of the Dominican Republic differed from those of adjoining Haiti by being of white stock. It is true that the white contribution to the racial mixture is greater in the Dominican Republic, but some 60 or 70 percent of the population has an identifiable proportion of African ancestry. Trujillo himself had a black grandmother from Haiti, a fact he tried to hide by powdering and painting his face. In any case, one of his inviolable diktats was that no photograph of a black Dominican should ever leave the country. And CUNA insisted on a photograph of the deceased before paying on the policy. I had to send the photograph, although the man was black, and I similarly sent photographs of several other blacks who died. Trujillo had all mails examined as a matter of course, and I received tips from friends that reports were going to the government about the photographs. However, as long as Peña Batlle was around, I felt secure. But after we were enjoying the CUNA insurance for about two years, he died. What should I do now? I went for advice to my lawyer, Dr. Efraín Reyes Duluc, who also held a government post, though a less important one than Peña Batlle. "You have to drop the insurance," he said. "You have too many people gunning for you, and if they catch you on currency manipulation, they will crucify you. Why don't you think of starting a local insurance program on your own, even on a small scale?"

I was now in a predicament. I had to make a major change without explaining my real reasons. I couldn't come out and say publicly that I had been breaking the law with the connivance of Peña Batlle. A violent opposition developed, led by some of my Scarboro colleagues. No doubt there was a mixture of reasons. The Scarboro Fathers, with few exceptions, had taken little interest in the cooperative movement, and most of them thought this kind of work alien to the missionary. They may have felt that the reputation of the Scarboro Society would be associated with an insurance program started by the local federation of credit unions and feared the potential scandal if things went wrong. There was no doubt that several credit unions had folded as a result of misuse of funds by treasurers, something almost inevitable in a society built on graft and gangsterdom, as was Trujillo's Dominican Republic. In addition one of the benefits of CUNA membership was an expense-paid trip for a delegate to meetings in the United States, and as none of the Dominicans in the movement spoke English, the delegate chosen each time was a Scarboro priest. For some of them, that was a decisive argument in favor of retaining membership.

The annual meeting of the federation at which the issue was to be decided was held in January 1958 in San Francisco de Macorís, a small town lacking hotel accommodations. I arrived there with my aides a few days ahead of time to arrange space in private homes for the 125 or 150 delegates. There was a cooperative store in the town with a meeting hall attached, and it included a small room where I had a cot for overnight visits. By nine o'clock on Monday morning the hall was full and the directors had assembled on the platform. As we were about to start, we were amazed to see three men wearing long white cassocks march up the aisle. They were three of my colleagues from the capital, and I learned later that the three had spent the night in the local convent's only guest room. When the issue of the insurance was reached on the agenda, one of them got up and did everything he could to obtain a negative vote. But the delegates never wavered. The motion was passed unanimously.

They didn't stop there, however. The next thing I knew the superior general was down from Canada, primed with all the accusations. He gave me a bad time at first, saying I was accused of being disloyal and unwilling to adjust myself to the reasonable wishes of my colleagues. I held my ground and he went off to investigate further for himself. What changed his mind I never did learn, although I suspect he must have been profoundly influenced by the French-Canadian priests working in the Cibao region. Although they were members of a different mission society, they were always my staunchest backers. In any case, he returned with my three chief opponents and told them in my presence to leave me alone and for the future look after their own affairs.

All through the 1950's, the cooperative movement had been growing not only in the Dominican Republic but all around the Caribbean. As far back as January 1953, Monsignor Luigi Ligutti, then head of the Rural Life movement in the United States, came to the Dominican Republic to take me with him to Manizales, Colombia, to attend the first international congress of all mainland Latin America and the Caribbean islands to deal with rural problems. The Manizales program was impressive. There were about fifty bishops and more than two hundred priests in evidence, as well as 350 delegates from some twenty-five countries. Among old friends I ran into there were Father William Gibbons and Father Fred McGuire. With Fred I exchanged reminiscences of our common experiences in a China that already seemed so far in the past as to have been an earlier incarnation. The conference participants were impressed with what I could report about the value of the cooperative movement. In 1953 we had more than thirty groups incorporated and an even bigger number in preparation, with a combined membership of ten or eleven thousand, and savings in the neighborhood of $200,000. Several of the delegates expressed interest in visiting the Dominican Republic or sending students for courses in the school we had opened the previous year, and some subsequently did so.

Two years later, a similar congress was held in Panama, and for the first time it included a three-day workshop devoted to adult education and cooperatives, which Monsignor Ligutti asked me to organize. I was lucky to get such outstanding speakers as Bishop John R. MacDonald of Antigonish, Jerry Voorhis, executive director of the Cooperative League of the United States, Father Manuel Foyaca, S.J., of Cuba, Puerto Rico's Secretary of Agriculture Conón Torres, Mother Alicia from Dominica, and Father John Sullivan from Jamaica. Two important proposals were approved in principle at this meeting: the creation of a Caribbean confederation of credit unions and cooperatives, and the enlargement of the training school in the Dominican Republic to take pupils from all over the region. Both proposals were ultimately implemented, though the latter in a different country and in a way none of us then contemplated.

International recognition was also promoted by publicity provided by the news media. As a result of a talk I gave at an annual meeting of CUNA in Atlantic City one year, articles were published about the cooperative movement in *Commonweal, Ensign,* the *Progressive,* and the *Catholic Digest.* The *Digest* then had a Spanish-language edition, so that its article was distributed in the Dominican Republic and elsewhere in Latin America. Some of my friends were upset, fearing a negative reaction from Trujillo and his henchmen when they read how important we had become. Nothing happened immediately, but possibly this was a factor in our final overthrow. What I remember at the time is my disappointment that all the publicity produced only a few hundred dollars in donations to meet our pressing debts. It did, however, bring many requests for information, even from as far away as Korea and the Philippines.

Clash with a Dictator

On the surface, everything was going splendidly for the cooperative movement. We had practically reached saturation point for credit unions in the Cibao, and they were also expanding elsewhere. The first marketing cooperative was incorporated at Yamasá in 1954, and it was followed by many marketing and consumer cooperatives. We were also experimenting with cooperative housing in the villages. Yet I was becoming more and more conscious of the shakiness of the foundations. It was not merely the opposition of the merchants, even though it was reinforced by significant elements among the clergy. Even worse was the growing tension and suspicion everywhere, the growing harshness of the police with the ordinary people, the growing arbitrariness of officials who one day promised something, then pulled the rug from under your feet the next day after you had committed yourself and spent your money.

Much of what happened in those years still escapes rational explanation. Trujillo was not only a dictator but a madman. There was no press freedom and no political parties. Trujillo had a finger in every business, and he insisted on getting a cut from every activity, lawful or unlawful. When people were squeezed, they squeezed others in turn almost as a reflex action. Everywhere one heard rumors of killings, tortures, exiling of suspects, extortions, robberies. Finally, in the late 1950's, the long-complacent Church raised its voice when the bishops got together and issued an open and strongly worded letter protesting the violations by the authorities of basic human rights. Trujillo lashed back, escalating the conflict. We were building up to the climax, the charge by Venezuela that Trujillo was plotting to kill its president, a charge sustained by the OAS in 1960, and the assassination of Trujillo himself in 1961.

The axe had fallen on the cooperative movement two years earlier, in 1959. I had gone to the United States and Canada on one of my frequent fund-raising trips. On the way back I stopped off at Puerto Rico to discuss some cooperative problems, checking in to the monastery of the Capuchin Fathers who were always happy to extend hospitality to me. I was not long there when a man came to the door and asked for me by name. He said he was a sailor who had signed on a ship at Tampico, Mexico, gone first to the Dominican Republic, and then come here on the same ship to Puerto Rico. He wanted money so that he could get back home, and he was also particularly anxious that I should accompany him to a restaurant for a meal. When I refused, he went off reluctantly and I noticed that he spent a long time studying the house from different angles, as a person might if he was thinking of breaking in.

I discussed the incident with some of the priests, and when we checked out the story, we found there was no such boat at the docks. The man had claimed to have been told in the Dominican Republic that he could find me at the Capuchin monastery in Puerto Rico, but in fact there was nobody there who knew my travel plans. It did not take us long to decide that my visitor was a Trujillo bullyboy and that I was under elaborate surveillance. That was not too surprising, because I had already had several warnings that Trujillo felt I was acquiring too much influence and power through the cooperative movement. I had even once been held for three hours at pistol point by the head of the army intelligence who wanted me to sign a statement implicating another officer. I was also aware that the long arm of the tyrant could reach out across the sea. There had been the abduction on the streets of New York of a Columbia University professor who had written a book critical of Trujillo, a man who disappeared forever without leaving a trace. Indeed, Trujillo took pride in his ingenious schemes that made assassinations look like accidents and left everyone guessing who had done what.

On top of the bogus sailor came a whole series of incidents which induced me to delay my departure for the Dominican Republic until the situation clarified. Through trustworthy intermediaries I got reports from the island and they all added up to the advice that if I valued my life, I should stay away. When my religious superiors were informed, they ordered me back to Canada. Then, overnight, the cooperative movement in the Dominican Republic began to fall apart. That was not simply because of my absence. In the Cibao, in particular, as later events have demonstrated, the roots had sunk deep. But the atmosphere of terror, which would continue for years, even after the death of Trujillo, was universal. There were six governments in the following four years, including a period of bloody civil war and an occupation of the island by United States marines in 1965. By the time all that had ended, many of the cooperative groups had dissolved and most of those that remained were in bad shape.

After some semblance of peace was restored in 1966, however, it quickly became clear that the movement was far from dead. The report of the annual meeting of the federation of credit unions for the year 1970, for example, listed ninety functioning credit unions. About that same time, Dr. Carlos Berger, who travels all over Latin America on behalf of the German aid-giving agency, Misereor, told me that as far away as Chile he had been told that the most solidly based cooperative movement in Latin America was in the Dominican Republic, the stated reason being the tradition of weekly study sessions.

I was able to confirm this for myself in 1971 when I had an opportunity to visit many of my old friends as a guest of the Dominican cooperative movement. Not only is there a federation of credit unions, but also federations of the various other major kinds of cooperative, marketing cooperatives, consumer cooperatives, and so on. Even transportation cooperatives are being developed, an essential link if consumer and marketing cooperatives are to escape the clutches of the middleman. All these federations are joined at the top through a national confederation. In addition, the government has set up a department to encourage and promote the cooperative movement, the Institute of Cooperative Development and Credit (IDECOOP).

Memories long faded were revived during this visit. Fifty members of the cooperative in El Guano came to a reunion in Santiago, recalling one of the most unusual of my experiences in the Dominican Republic. In 1952, a woman sought me out at Altigracia on one of my visits to the Cibao. She identified herself as the sacristan of a small chapel at a place called El Guano. She had heard about the cooperatives and felt that this was what the village needed. At her urging, I went there on horseback. There was then no road, no school, no resident priest. It was one of the most isolated places I ever saw. The hundred or more men who came to listen to me all looked alike, inbred for generations, small, undernourished. Only three or four could read or write, but they were highly intelligent. They were sharecroppers, working small plots of land in primitive conditions and far from markets. But they were ready to learn. I went back each month for a discussion session. Then one of those who could read came to Santiago and stayed long enough to learn to keep books. They started a credit union and subsequently a consumer cooperative and stayed with them through thick and thin. In commercial terms, the whole operation is of small import. The latest report shows 101 members in the credit union, with savings of $7,381 and 42 current loans for a total of $4,543. But these trivial figures were given a different dimension for me by the men who told me at Santiago, with tears in their eyes, that more than once in years of drought they would have died of hunger were it not for the credit union and the store. So narrow are the margins with which these people cling to life that survival may hang on the availability of two dollars. Having established their credit-worthiness through participation in the cooperative, they could count on credit that was formerly denied them.

The cooperative movement in the Dominican Republic, nevertheless, is still far from a condition of normal health and progress. Some of its problems are those that block the movement's progress everywhere in Latin America, while others are special to the country itself. One of the latter is the psychological situation resulting from Trujillo's long dictatorship and the following years of turmoil. Perhaps the cruelest blow was the United States intervention in 1965. It was not primarily the destruction of life and property caused by the massive fire power of the occupying force, although the well-established practice of destroying one's friends in the act of saving them was once again verified on this occasion. The biggest problem was that the artificial separation of the opposing internal forces prevented the reestablishment of the equilibrium shattered by Trujillo. There is still unfinished business in the blood of the people, so many families nursing the bitter injustices they had suffered, remembering daughters raped and sons slaughtered. These are family issues which outside interference only aggravates. And on top of that, the end result of the intervention was to restore to power the very same army that had served Trujillo so faithfully and so ruthlessly. Even the president elected in 1966 and similarly elected in 1970 is the same Joaquín Balaguer who was for many years one of Trujillo's top lieutenants and who was awarded the presidency by him in 1960.

Now I happen to have considerable admiration for Balaguer. He is not a cruel man. I believed he saved hundreds of lives while he worked with Trujillo. Even his enemies distinguish between his regime and that of Trujillo by making a pun on the Spanish word for dictatorship, *dictadura,* saying that his regime is a *dicta-blanda,* not a *dicta-dura,* that is to say, a mild dictatorship, not a harsh one like Trujillo's. But the military still control and they still tyrannize the country, using him as a front man. I was told that the wealthy are in league with the army to repress every popular movement and syphon off the wealth created by the peasants. By 1971 they had followed the leadership of Guatemala and Brazil by sponsoring a nationwide network of vigilantes to protect the rich against the poor. Known in the Dominican Republic as *la banda* (the band), these thugs are generously paid and well armed, and they have a wide discretion to roam the countryside terrorizing and beating respectable people, and assassinating their critics. The general intention is similar to that of Trujillo, namely, to ensure a sense of fear and powerlessness in the face of injustice.

Naturally, neither cooperatives nor any other movement based on justice and merit can thrive in such a climate. But the negative impact is even more direct.

For example, when coffee marketing cooperatives were started a few years ago, they were given an export quota of 4,000 bags, and this meant that the cooperative members were getting four times as much per bag for their product as when they sold to the local middlemen. This experience encouraged a rapid expansion of coffee marketing cooperatives, and they now produce some 25,000 bags a year. In the meantime, however, the middlemen got together with government officials to readjust the quotas. They kept 70 percent of the total for themselves and gave most of the balance to big growers, leaving a quota of only 2,000 bags for the cooperatives. The result is that they still have to sell nearly the whole of their production to the middlemen at the prices they choose to pay, so that they are back almost where they started.

Another problem, and one that unfortunately exists in many other places also, is that government interference tends to distort the principles of the movement. Actually, there is no easy solution. The cooperative movement is far more than a technique for saving money and exchanging goods. The economic principles developed by Rochdale and the moral principles added by Antigonish require the total education of the members through the development of the concepts of justice, equity, trust, solidarity, thrift, and all the natural virtues. It is an adult education process that must continue through many years. When those involved are people of limited educational background and resources, they need outside help for a long time. Since the end result will benefit not only the members but the entire community, it is proper that the public authorities help, not only by legislation favoring cooperatives but by setting up a department or institute charged with encouraging and promoting the movement.

All this has been done in the Dominican Republic. The Institute of Cooperative Development and Credit was created in 1963 and has since grown into an impressive bureaucracy with headquarters in the capital and field workers in all parts of the country. The natural tendency of every bureaucracy, however, is to control even when its mandate is to encourage. There has consequently developed an emotional split between the "independent" movement which had grown up in poverty with minimum government recognition or help and the "official" movement which is able to subsidize its friends liberally, pay far higher salaries to its field workers, and get administrative preference in competitive situations. While many of the employees are well trained in cooperative principles, there is always the temptation in bureaucratic situations to rule from above. The long preparatory period of education is neglected, and thus the directors and employees lack a grounding in the cooperatives' principles, a grounding which is essential if they are to gain the proper motivation. The result is to produce capitalist business enterprises disguised as cooperatives, as so often happens also in the United States and other developed countries, and to produce credit unions for business groups or government employees which are really part of the banking system, a convenience and saving certainly for their members but something far less than the start toward the new man and the new society which are the goal of the true cooperative movement.

This distortion and emasculation of the movement is most evident in a program sponsored by United States foreign aid. In 1969, the United States authorities authorized a loan of $2,650,000 "to strengthen the cooperative movement in the Dominican Republic." The intention was that $2,000,000 would be available to make loans, principally to production and marketing cooperatives, to help increase agricultural production. The balance was intended for the salaries and expenses of technical advisers and loan administrators. It soon emerged, however, that the overriding purpose was not to increase agricultural production in the Dominican Republic but to encourage the farmers to get into crops that would not compete with those of which the United States has a surplus either at home or from other sources. Specifically, no loans could be made for rice, coffee, or light tobacco.

The next disclosure was that the technical advisers would be experts, not in agronomy, which is where help is most needed, but in the limited area of account keeping and marketing. In spite of the availability of many qualified Dominicans, the United States authorities insisted on bringing in United States citizens from Puerto Rico and the mainland as technical advisers and administrators. Next, the loans were limited to a period of one year or less, for the purpose of helping in the production or marketing of a single crop. The red tape in which the technical advisers and administrators wrapped the loan packages was such that at the end of two years, less than half a million dollars had been allocated. And since loans are always for a period of not more than one year, this means that the superstructure of United States technical advisers and administrators must remain on location for the entire twenty years of the loan's duration.

What it all adds up to is a long-term control of the direction to be taken by the cooperative movement in the Dominican Republic and considerable leverage over the country's agricultural policy, all at no net cost to the United States. In addition, many Dominicans recall the links between the CIA and other elements of the United States presence both in the Dominican Republic and elsewhere in Latin America, and they read into this project an ingenious device for grassroots espionage in the Dominican Republic. But as long as the country has an unrepresentative government which remains in power through the support of the United States, no effective protest is possible.

While such external obstacles remain, the cooperative movement can never realize its full potential. Unfortunately, as we shall see in later chapters, the Dominican Republic is in this respect a microcosm of all Latin America.

4

PANAMA

Side Trip to British Guiana

One thing remained clear in my mind through all the confusion and disappointment of the Dominican Republic debacle. The cooperative idea could work in Latin America wherever it was given half a chance. And there was nothing that Latin America needed more than cooperatives. All the efforts to bring development to the region would fail as long as the people were left on the margin of the action. Only the Latin Americans themselves, the millions of the dispossessed poor, could build a new society. And the cooperative movement offered a proven method of adult education and self-reliance to start the people on that road. As Father Coady once said, "the common man is capable." It is our job to provide for him the opportunity to create the kind of society in which he will be "free to free his soul."

The Scarboro Fathers had taken on another mission in Latin America while I was in the Dominican Republic. They went to British Guiana (now Guyana) in 1953, the same year in which the British granted that colony partial independence. The seeds of trouble had been sown in British Guiana in the nineteenth century. When the freed slaves refused to continue to work on the old terms for their former masters, the British imported coolies from India to cut the sugar cane. Their descendants, known as East Indians, had grown by the 1950's to constitute slightly more than half the population. They had stayed mostly in the country, whereas the blacks and other elements in the very mixed population lived in and around the capital, Georgetown. The East Indians were very poor and largely illiterate, but they were socially cohesive and were determined not to remain indefinitely at the bottom of the social and economic pile. All the elements of bitter conflict were present.

In elections held in 1953, the People's Progressive Party, led by Cheddi Jagan, an East Indian dentist-turned-politician, won a majority. Jagan and his American-born wife were self-declared Marxists, and they quickly initiated a series of radical reforms which frightened the business community and led the British to suspend the constitution and reoccupy the territory. Order was restored, but the underlying tensions continued, with divisions following strictly racial lines, Jagan solidly backed by the East Indians on one side, and the rest of the community on the other. Many reforms were instituted in an effort to lessen the appeal of Jagan's Marxist platform, and I was happy to comply when I was invited to see what role cooperatives might play. That the movement can contribute to lessening social tension has been demonstrated beyond challenge. But the political instability of the territory and the mounting unrest gave little hope of any significant development for the foreseeable future. It seemed clear that Jagan would regain power at the elections scheduled for 1961, as in fact he did, and that a long period of internecine strife and violence would follow, as in fact also occurred. I felt no desire to get involved in a situation that might end up like the one I had just experienced in the Dominican Republic. But I had an even more basic reason for not wanting to establish myself in a location that was English-speaking and that was not easy to reach from many parts of the continent. What I was now planning was a single international institution to train leaders for the many countries whose language was Spanish. It ought to be in a city that was both Spanish-speaking and highly accessible. I accordingly returned to Canada in 1961.

Membership in the Scarboro Society had enabled me to do many things that would otherwise have been difficult or impossible. I never lost sight of that fact, and one of the reasons I treasure the priesthood and membership in the Society is the freedom it provides me to dedicate myself to my missionary calling. But not all my colleagues saw my vocation as proper to the Scarboro Society. For them, the missionary should preach the truths of religion, baptize, say Mass, administer the sacraments. They could not see the relation between the message of Christ and my concern to help men create for themselves a material base on which they could build dignity, self-respect, freedom to make their own decisions, the freedom without which a man is unable to posit a human act, unable to act morally, or for that matter, immorally.

My plan to develop an international institute to train cooperative leaders in Latin America raised all these issues for the Society's superiors. It was still only 1961, several years before the Vatican Council would even begin to draft the Constitution on the Church in the Modern World. There was little precedent for what I proposed. So I was not surprised to find that an answer was likely to take some time. I settled into a job as chaplain in a small hospital in Toronto, proceeded to read every book on cooperatives and on social justice I could find, started to write a textbook on social action, and kept up a steady pressure for a decision. Some points gradually clarified themselves. I was offered jobs in the cooperative movement by the governments of Puerto Rico and of Venezuela. My superiors decided that working for a government would not be appropriate for a member of Scarboro. I did not want to leave the Society, and I was not enthusiastic about working for a government, so it created no real problem for me to decline the offers. But one benefit resulted from the discussions. It became clear that Scarboro would be less negative if I could find some church institution to sponsor me.

In August 1962, I began my exploration by visiting several friends in the United States. Following the Vatican's appeal to the churches of Western Europe and North America to send 10 percent of their personnel to work in Latin America during the 1960's, delegates of the bishops of Latin America and those of North America met in 1960 and decided to set up a secretariat for Latin America attached to the United States Bishops' Conference. Its first director was Father John Considine, a Maryknoller. A little later, an organization known as the Papal Volunteers for Latin America (PAVLA) was set up under the auspices of the United States bishops to encourage and help the training and allocation of lay Catholics who wanted to participate in church programs in Latin America. There was then great enthusiasm for a movement which paralleled the recently created Peace Corps.

Father Considine had spent a week with me in the Dominican Republic seven years earlier, including a trip to the Cibao to see the change being wrought by the cooperatives, which he recorded in his book *New Horizons in Latin America*. I had no difficulty in persuading him of the value of my project. "But before you decide where to locate," he said, "I think you should take a trip to all the countries bordering on the Caribbean."

I agreed. It would give me a chance to make a complete comparison. We drew up a plan "for the formation of a corps of lay social experts assisted by priests, to work in Latin America." The approval of Father Considine as director of the Latin American secretariat of the United States bishops was all my superiors wanted. They immediately released me from other duties to dedicate myself to this. A personal friend, an American business-man who prefers to remain anonymous in his good deeds, financed my trip, not only to the Caribbean countries but to all twenty Latin American republics. It was to occupy six months.

The experience was enormously enriching, although I would not advise anyone to repeat it literally. Two months on the road is more than enough. Different places, different people, and different languages build up to a point of emotional exhaustion. It is better to take a piece at a time, then pause for digestion. But I achieved my principal purpose. I came back with a list of two hundred people who were interested in socioeconomic issues and in a position to exercise an influence on the direction in which their countries are moving. About half the list consisted of priests, also some bishops. The lay people covered a broad spectrum of ideological positions, includ-ing quite a few labeled as Communists. The label was loosely used by many to describe anyone seeking social change, but it was clear to me that some thinkers were being pushed farther to the left each year by the rigidity of the power structures. I was struck by the intensity of feeling against the United States in several countries, especially such major countries as Chile, Argentina, and Brazil. The ugly image was not confined to government officials and businessmen, but spilled over also on priests and nuns from the United States, who were seen as uncon-sciously promoting the policies and spreading the culture of their homeland. All these negative tendencies have, of course, been further intensified and more publicly expressed in subsequent years.

Most Latin American churchmen, especially bishops, seemed completely oblivious of what was going on around them, remote, uninvolved, playing medieval games. But some offered a striking contrast, men whose names were soon to become internationally known: Manuel Larraín of Talca, Chile; Eugenio Sales of Natal, Brazil; Helder Camara, then in Rio and later moved to Recife, Brazil; Ramón Bogarín of Paraguay; Mark McGrath of Panama; Antonio Fragoso of Crateus, Brazil; Sergio Méndez Arceo of Cuernavaca, Mexico.

My last stop on my way home was for three weeks in the Dominican Republic. A year had passed since Trujillo's assassination, and Juan Bosch had been elected president. People were breathing and speaking more freely, although nobody thought that all the problems of the past had been laid to rest. For me it was a pleasant surprise to find that some elements of the cooperative movement had survived in the Cibao, about forty credit unions and six consumer stores. Everywhere I went the people wanted me to return and resume where I had left off. I did not feel I could tell them why I was unwilling, but when the newly appointed papal nuncio, Archbishop Emanuale Clarizio, made the same request, I did tell him straight out. The previous year, after Trujillo was killed, Father Frank Diemert, superior general of the Scarboro Fathers, had asked me if I wanted to go back to the Dominican Republic. We agreed that he should first find out what the bishops down there thought, because in the confused situation I would need their moral support. By this time, my friend, Archbishop Pittini, had died. Father Diemert wrote to all five bishops, but received an answer from only one of them, and it was a devious one. "If the bishops don't want me," I told the nuncio, "Why should I waste my time?" He was displeased, but I stood my ground. Undoubtedly it was better that way. Within six months Bosch was overthrown and exiled by the military, starting a new round of terror. The only bishop I visited was the old and blind Spanish Capuchin at La Vega, Francisco Panal Ramírez.

On my return I spent ten days in Washington, where I discussed in detail my impressions with Father Considine and with my friend from China days, Father Fred Maguire, who was now head of the mission secretariat. One basic issue that was raised was why set up a new institute when Antigonish was already providing the same kind of course and had achieved a worldwide reputation. Would it not be less expensive and more efficient simply to send trainees there? Naturally, I had no wish to question the authority of Antigonish, but my experience in Latin America had convinced me that it was not the answer. Over the years I had talked with dozens of Latin Americans while they were studying at Antigonish and after they returned home. For most of them, living in Antigonish was difficult. They could not adjust to the customs, the food, and the cold weather. The language was a particular problem. Most of the Asian and African students had a solid command of English, while few Latin Americans were at home in it, and some had to start from scratch. In consequence, a Latin American who had a doctorate in economics might find himself at the bottom of a class, outranked by Asians and Africans who had never gone beyond high school. The result was many emotional distortions and frustrations. Some came back embittered against the entire cooperative movement, and never made any use of their new knowledge.

From Washington, at the urging of Monsignor William J. Quinn, I went to Chicago. Monsignor Quinn was responsible for migrant workers and for the PAVLA program in the archiocese of Chicago. He was also connected with Father Considine's office, and he was engaged in developing the Catholic Inter-American Cooperation Program (CICOP) whose annual conferences were to play an important part in the relations between the Church in Latin America and the United States in subsequent years. Monsignor Quinn was emphatic that Chicago was the best place in the United States to establish a base from which I could enlist support for the major training center I had in mind. Under the leadership of Albert Cardinal Meyer, who had come there from Milwaukee in 1958, it had acquired the reputation of being the most progressive Catholic area in the United States. I had been leaning toward Boston because I had met Richard Cardinal Cushing several times and because his admiration for Antigonish and his concern for Latin America were well known. In favor of Chicago, nevertheless, was the presumption that a broad-based movement could be created there, whereas in Boston the support would be personal and would not survive the Cardinal himself.

Another area I checked out as a potential base was Madison, Wisconsin, where the United States foreign aid program had recently funded an International Cooperative Training Center in connection with the University of Wisconsin. The man who had originated the idea was my good friend, Jerry Voorhis. I had first met Jerry at a meeting of CUNA in 1953, and he was then already well known for his pioneer work in promoting cooperatives both in the United States and internationally. He was, in fact, about to go to Antigonish to receive an honorary degree at the ceremonies for the centenary of the university in May 1953. Jerry, a New Deal Democrat, had earlier been a congressman from California, until he was defeated in 1946 by a political newcomer backed by big business who charged that he was "soft on communism." The newcomer: Richard Milhous Nixon. Although I knew I could always count on Jerry's personal support, I did not think I would gain much by setting up my base in Wisconsin. The courses were far too theoretical for my purposes.

When I returned to Canada at the end of May 1963, after nearly ten months of constant travel in Latin America and the United States, I thought I had a definite program lined up. I had made contact with Bishop James MacManus of Ponce and Father John Mueller, rector of the Catholic University of Puerto Rico in Ponce, and both of them were anxious that I should establish my cooperative training center at Ponce in connection with the Catholic University, the bishop offering me a part of the seminary rent-free to start me off. What seemed to me most promising was to try first to establish a base in Chicago, where I would both raise money and recruit young North Americans prepared to work in the cooperative movement in Latin America. Ivan Illich, then vice-rector of the Catholic University at Ponce, had operated a language school there. It had closed when he pulled out in 1960 as a result of his public clash with the bishops of Puerto Rico for denouncing the birth-control policies of Governor Luis Muñoz Marín and trying to block his reelection. It was, however, planned to reopen it in August 1963, and I could send the North Americans there for language training and in due course also bring Latin Americans to Ponce to train as cooperative leaders.

Things, nevertheless, did not run as smoothly as I anticipated. I had hoped to recruit two or three people at Antigonish to form the nucleus of a staff at Ponce. Monsignor Frank Smyth was friendly and warmly encouraged me, something I had not anticipated, but he had his own staff difficulties and could make no practical contribution. Bishop William Power, a Montrealer, who was named to head the diocese of Antigonish in 1960, was polite but noncommittal. Within a month I went back to Chicago with the intention of setting up a permanent base there, and hoping that by the following January I would be able to start a six-month course in Ponce. Monsignor Quinn gave me temporary office space in the PAVLA offices and also found me living quarters in the rectory of St. Carthage parish. St. Carthage was the most unusual rectory I ever saw. The pastor, Father John Hayes, was about my own age, a saintly man but in failing health. The neighborhood was typical of the Chicago inner-city, all poor blacks just up from the South, crime-infested, without sanitation or street-cleaning services, ignored by the police. Every night, cars were damaged on the streets, and it was dangerous to move about after dark. The rectory had no cook, with the only formal meal each day prepared by a high-school student. Her repertoire was limited to pork and hamburgers, far too rich for my ulcer-prone stomach. And of course there was no restaurant within miles.

The contacts with PAVLA failed to bring the benefits I had hoped. There were six or seven priests working in the same building with me, and Monsignor Quinn had me sit in at a quarterly meeting of the organization when eight or ten priests came together from around the country. But not one of them showed the slightest interest in my work or offered any concrete help. I would have felt hopelessly isolated but for two people, Elaine Kup, who was Monsignor Quinn's secretary, and a dynamic young layman from England, Dave O'Shea, who was on the PAVLA staff. But what the two of them could do for me was very limited because of the lack of interest higher up. So I was forced to start my own independent publicity program, hiring a public-relations firm to prepare the materials. We mailed out 45,000 brochures to lists obtained from various Catholic organizations, and we got some stories into newspapers and magazines about our proposed Inter-American Cooperative Institute (ICI), the name with which we have remained. It has the advantage of having the same initials in Spanish,

Instituto Cooperativo Interamericano, as in English. Subsequently, ICI was incorporated as a nonprofit organization in the State of New York, with Father John Catoir as chairman of the board of directors, a position he continues to occupy. I first met Jack Catoir in the early 1950's when he was a seminarian in his second year of theology. He came on a visit to the Dominican Republic and we were brought together by a mutual friend. He joined with me on several field trips and quickly became enthusiastic about the work I was doing to promote the cooperative movement. His enthusiasm and our friendship have since continued. I can at all times count on him to carry out with dispatch and efficiency any task in the United States I entrust to him.

While working out of the PAVLA office in Chicago, I was helped for a time by Father Pancratius Conway, a Franciscan who was on a sabbatical leave after twenty years' work as a missionary in Costa Rica. He was very enthusiastic at the beginning, but he soon reached the conclusion that I could not succeed, and he left me. By this time, I had met Cardinal Meyer, who authorized me to open an office in the archdiocese, provided I didn't want from him "either money or priests." I also met the Pat Crowleys, who headed the Christian Family Movement, and leaders of Young Christian Workers, Young Christian Students, and other Catholic groups. Everywhere I got polite words but little understanding and no commitment. The publicity brought several potential helpers, some priests, some lay people. I explored at least half a dozen, some at considerable expense, but not a single one worked out.

This was perhaps the most frustrating year in my life. As the time approached for the course I had planned to give in Ponce, the three prospective students all changed their minds. The head of the overseas program of CUNA asked me to take charge of a program to be

financed through Washington's foreign aid, which would
have involved the setting up of a credit-union training
school in Costa Rica. However, he lost his job while
the negotiations with the foreign-aid people in Washington
were still in progress, and his successor seemed to have
no interest in pursuing the project, so that I finally decided
it was hopeless. By a curious coincidence I subsequently
got to know very well the man who was later appointed
to head this program. He was Herb Wegner, and he established his home and his headquarters in Panama for
several years while doing a magnificent job of promotion
of credit unions in Latin America. I was already located
in Panama, as will be explained shortly, when he came
there. Both Herb and his wife took a great interest in
my work, and they helped me in more ways than I could
recount right up to the time when he returned to the
United States in 1971 to head up the domestic operations
of CUNA in Madison, Wisconsin.

While I was in Washington in 1963 trying to get a decision from the foreign-aid people on the CUNA project
for Latin America, I met Congressman John McCor-
mack, Speaker of the House, Teodoro Moscoso, head
of the AID program for Latin America, James Roosevelt,
and Sergeant Shriver, head of the Peace Corps. All of
them seemed positively interested in what I wanted to
do, but no action followed. Time and again I contemplated
the wisdom of giving up altogether my plan to found
an inter-American cooperative institute. What kept me
going was not so much my reluctance to return to Scarboro a failure, as the prospect of sitting there in idleness
for the rest of my life. That I could not contemplate.

What was becoming gradually clearer to me was that
neither the Church nor the government of the United
States was going to give me the money I needed to start
the institute. And that seemed to mean that I would be
forced to abandon the idea entirely. No alternative source

for the substantial amount involved seemed visible in any quarter. But, in retrospect, when I see the subtle distortions caused to Latin American institutions by the conditions under which those kind of funds were given to them, I am happy I had to suffer and do it all the hard way. Most of the money I have received from the United States was contributed by personal friends, and always with no strings attached. In 1969 and subsequent years I was helped generously by the Division for Latin America of the United States Catholic Conference. But I was already well started before that help came. In addition, the head of the Bureau at that time was Father Louis Michael Colonnese, a man whose views on Latin America and its relationship to the United States closely paralleled my own.

It was one of these personal friends who now came to my aid with an offer to underwrite a trial course in a Latin American country. The two sites that seemed most promising were Costa Rica and Panama, and in the end I opted for Panama. While on my tour the previous year, I had met Bishop Mark McGrath, auxiliary to Archbishop Francis Beckmann of Panama City, and he had shown considerable enthusiasm for my plan. But even more than on him, I counted on Porfirio Gómez, head of the national land reform program. I first met Porfirio at the Social Action Congress held in Panama in 1955. He was then a regional director for FAO in the Caribbean, having previously held a similar post in Japan. Then in 1963, we met again in a hotel in El Salvador. He was at that time working for the United Nations in El Salvador. We got to talking about the need for the kind of land reform which had been made official policy by all the nations of the hemisphere at their recent meeting at Punta del Este, thanks to the initiatives of President John F. Kennedy. I told Porfirio this was his chance to do something great for his own country, Panama, namely, to go home and develop an official policy and program. "I'll do that," he said, "if you promise to come to Panama too and set up your cooperative institute there. Together, we could transform the country." In any case, without waiting for a formal undertaking from me, which I was not in a position to give him, Porfirio did return home and had himself named to head up the land reform institute. He was delighted when he learned that I might in fact be coming to Panama, and he sent me a cable urging a quick decision. I also heard from Oscar Monteza, who had been to Antigonish and knew the value of the cooperative movement.

Putting all these factors together, I decided to try Panama. I had about fifteen students lined up from Ecuador, Honduras, Guatemala, El Salvador, Mexico, the United States, and Panama, and Father John Kennedy, C.M., who headed up Caritas in Panama, arranged with the Salesian Fathers to allow me to use their technical school for the months of February and March, which would give time to find alternative accommodations for the rest of the course. In January 1964, just as we were ready to start, fierce rioting broke out over the failure of the United States to abide by an agreement, made after some riots in 1959, to display both Panamanian and United States flags simultaneously in the Canal Zone. At least twenty people died, including three United States soldiers, and hundreds were injured. Diplomatic relations with the United States were interrupted for several months. The riots were a factor in delaying the start of the course for two weeks, but we did open on February 17, 1964, in a situation that was still explosive. For once, my Canadian citizenship was a decided benefit. The course received a lot of newspaper, radio, and television coverage, when seven students were beaten up and five of them hospitalized, and the number of pupils grew to thirty-five full-time and fifteen part-time. Verbal support for the work came from a group of conservative businessmen who loudly proclaimed their Catholicism but whose real driving force was the terror they felt for what they called "the communist menace." That simply meant a determination to maintain the status quo. They hoped that an organization headed by a priest would help to keep the peasants in line.

While pleased with the success of this first course in Panama, I was very much conscious of the shallowness of my base. I needed a major grant to build and equip a center, as well as the continuing guarantee of funds to maintain it. An institution of this kind cannot be self-sustaining without distorting its purpose, because the people who need to be trained are the very poor who can least afford such luxuries. Once it is well established and has created a reputation for excellence, some governments will pay the cost of training for people working in national departments or institutes for the promotion of the cooperative movement. But even then, it is essential to service also the grassroots cooperative groups of limited income, and even more those who are struggling without funds or official support to make a start.

Accordingly, I went straight back to Chicago when the course ended, bought a car, and started a long trek all through the Midwest and Northeast of the United States and up into Canada as far as Antigonish, driving as much as 800 miles in a single day. The results were as disappointing as before. Even in the diocese of Antigonish, which traditionally has a surplus of priests and is willing to lend some to worthy mission causes, I found little or no response, and there was the same kind of apathy elsewhere in Canada and the United States. It was clear that the official Church was not interested in the kind of approach I was offering. As before, the only money I got was from some private individuals. Without them I could not have continued.

Vatican Council Opens New Vistas

By this time we were in the third year of the Vatican Council, and a lot of the things I had been thinking privately for many years about the mission of the Church and the need to identify with the cause of the poor and downtrodden were being spoken and written about openly in the most orthodox quarters. I decided to visit Rome during the third session, which was scheduled to start in mid-September. In that way, I could get some idea of the direction of progressive thinking and meet important people, especially bishops from Latin America who would be in a position to influence in my favor the aid-giving churches of Europe and North America.

On my way to Rome I went for a few days to Belgium to meet August Vanistandael and other leaders of the Christian Democratic movement in Europe who were interested in promoting social justice in Latin America, especially to the extent that objective could be combined with a credit to the Social Democrats in Latin America, whose prospects for winning with presidential candidate Eduardo Frei looked very good as the 1964 Chilean elections drew near. Vanistandael was president of the International Confederation of Christian Trade Unions, a labor movement closely related to the Christian Democrats and represented in Latin America by unions affiliated to the Confederacion Latinoamericana de Sindicalistas Cristianos (CLASC). He was also an adviser to the Vatican for the development of aid programs to poor countries and would be named one of the original members of the Vatican's Justice and Peace Commission when it was created shortly after the end of the Council. All these European Christian Democrats, as well as the Vatican, had poured money into Chile during the previous couple of years to block the socialist candidate and ensure the victory of Frei, a project in which they were all involved alongside the CIA. They continued to spend money freely in Latin America in subsequent years. But they concentrated on short-term political goals, including control of the labor movement. While the cooperative movement got some help from them and continues to do so, the amount is insignificant.

Monsignor William Quinn was able to arrange to have me stay at Villanova House in Rome, where there were twenty-five United States bishops, as well as a smaller number from France, Belgium, and Italy. We also had a number of the theological advisers, or *periti,* including John Courtney Murray and Hans Küng, who were responsible for our hostel becoming known as the House of Rebels. Bishop Ernest Primeau of Manchester, New Hampshire, was a kind of unofficial host. Other United States bishops that I got to know well included Walter Curtis of Bridgeport, Connecticut, and Charles Helmsing of Kansas City, Missouri. They were kept quite busy most of the time, with Council sessions in St. Peter's in the morning and committee meetings in the afternoon. But often in the evening we would gather for a talk session which ranged over the day's happenings and the general thrust of the Council, usually with Bishop Primeau acting as sparring partner, to get the discussion moving, with Monsignor George Higgins of the Social Action Department of the United States Bishops' Conference.

While much of these informal exchanges did not go beyond the details of political infighting and the underhand maneuvering at which the Curia in particular was a past master, certain broad directions were emerging which gave me considerable interior satisfaction. For one thing, there was coming into the open a whole new questioning of the missionary effort of the past two or three centuries. People were talking openly about the Chinese Rites, which we had had to take an oath never to discuss when we landed in China in 1938. They were reaching the same conclusion which I had long ago reached as a result of my discussions with Father Aaron Gignac and Father Desmond Stringer, namely, that the decision of the Roman Curia to condemn the efforts of the early Jesuit missionaries to give Christianity in China a Chinese dress and manner had been one of the Church's greatest blunders of all time.

Coming right up to the twentieth century, they were beginning to wonder what would happen to the Church in Asia and Africa as a result of the ending of the colonial era. It was easy to explain why the Communists in China expelled the foreign missionaries and dragooned the local bishops and priests into cutting ties with Rome. That was how earlier Communists had treated the Church in Russia and Eastern Europe. But it was less easy to understand why India, Ceylon, and Indonesia had introduced a parallel policy of restricting the entry of foreign missionaries, or why the new countries of Africa wanted to get control of the schools, hospitals, and other institutions with which the Christian missionaries had enriched their countries. And while all kinds of explanations and sociological projections were being offered, some responsible Church leaders were finally coming out and asserting publicly that Christian missionaries had often been the forerunners of the imperialists and their privileged servants, and that they could not hope to survive in the newly freed countries of the poor world unless they could show by deeds that they were not a rearguard for the withdrawing imperialists and a possible fifth column left behind to prepare their return.

One point that was becoming increasingly clear was that the emerging countries would insist on removing from the control of foreign missionaries the health, education, and welfare services they had built up with the support of the former colonial countries. In countries whose economy permitted such services for only a minority of the citizens, it was inevitable that the government would reserve to itself the selection of the beneficiaries. That meant that there would be no more rice Christians. It knocked out one of the major props of the old system. In broader terms, we were facing a situation in which Western culture could no longer be the vehicle for Christianity's expansion, and in which the decision-making processes in the former mission territories would have to be rapidly placed in the hands of local priests and missionaries. This conclusion was being forced on the bishops as a result of the converging impact of two different kinds of arguments. On the one side, there was the practical realization resulting from a study of the politcal facts that no other approach was viable. On the other, the new understanding of the nature of the Church which was leading toward the proclamation of çollegiality as its basic principle of authority was throwing a fresh light on the importance of the local church and its autonomous life. It meant that the local clergy, not the missionaries, should in the future be the guardians of spiritual values, and that these local clergy should be steeped in their own cultures and equipped to interpret the faith in the light of those cultures.

I do not think that many of the North American bishops had much awareness of all these radical changes in thinking or much realization that the end result would affect them. As far as they were concerned, these were largely intellectual exercises in which their European colleagues were engaged, and if they wanted to perform a ritual of public penance for their past sins, that was their affair. The North Americans were notoriously silent during the debate, at which by chance I was present, on a proposed decree on the missions. It was the only occasion on which Pope Paul intervened personally in a Council discussion and he asked specifically for a vote of approval of the text drafted and submitted by a Curia-dominated committee. In an unusual show of independence, the Council rejected the draft as unduly narrow and legalistic, and sent it back to committee to be rewritten.

Some of the Latin American bishops, with whom I spent much of my time, had a better appreciation than the North Americans of what was involved in all of this. Several of them were members of the "Church of the Poor" group set up at the first session of the Council in 1962 to help voice the needs and desires of those elements in the Church which had hitherto been unrepresented in the decision-making processes. Significantly, this group did not include a single representative of the hierarchies of any of the Anglo-Saxon countries, and the dominant feeling among the United States bishops was that its purpose was to rebuke them for living affluently or to act as a pressure group to extract from them a higher level of aid to the missions. The Church-of-the-Poor group did, nevertheless, play a vital part at the Council and was instrumental in starting processes that led to such subsequent breakthroughs as Pope Paul's encyclical on the development of the poor countries, *Populorum progressio,* the 1967 Letter to the Peoples of the Third World, signed by eighteen bishops from various poor countries, which called on the Church "to dispense the word of truth and the gospel of justice in its entirety," and the 1968 Medellín Documents in which the bishops of Latin America condemned both the "internal neocolonialism" and the "international monopolies and the international imperialism of money."

Ultimately, however, what for me held the greatest interest was the document, bitterly contested and many times rewritten, which was to emerge as the Constitution on the Church in the Modern World. Here was formalized the issue which I had debated back in China with the priest who sat in his rocking chair on his verandah in Lishui, and which had been a bone of contention between

me and many of my colleagues not only in the Scarboro
Society but in the ministry ever since. What is the function
of the priest and the missionary? More basically, what
is the function of the Church? Do we "save our souls"
by rocking on a balcony in China or Haiti or wherever?
Do we save the souls of others by baptizing them, hearing
their confessions, praying over their graves? Or is there
something more to the grand design of God? Yes, the
Council affirmed, there is considerably more. While pro-
claiming that man has a higher destiny, one so much
more important than his transitory life on earth that all
his judgments must be made in relation to it, it insisted—in
a Teilhardian perspective—that faith does not lessen the
Christian's commitment to man's progress on earth,
because his final destiny can be achieved only by due
concern for earthly activities. "The Church sincerely pro-
fesses that all men, believers and unbelievers alike, ought
to work for the rightful betterment of this world in which
all alike live." Human activity directed to the improvement of living conditions "accords with God's will. For
man, created to God's image, received a mandate to subject to himself the earth and all it contains . . . This
mandate concerns the whole of everyday activity . . .
The triumphs of the human race are a sign of God's
grace and a flowering of his mysterious design."

Getting down to a more concrete level, the document
reaffirmed the principle that man's control of nature is
now such that he is capable of satisfying the reasonable
needs of the entire human family, then drew the conclusion that justice demanded the giving of top priority to
ending the current monstrous economic inequalities both
within nations and between the rich nations and the poor
ones. Economic progress should not be used to
accumulate power or profits but to serve men without
distinction of race or geographic location. Private property has to be subordinated to this overriding objective,

and it cannot be presented as an obstacle to public ownership when such ownership is required by the common
good. The existence of huge landholdings in countries
in which rural masses are landless and starving is a
specific example of the abuse of private property. It is
the function of mankind, with the loyal and disinterested
help of the Church, to create a world in which the average
man everywhere will be able to live with dignity and
in comfort, in which men and nations will have a democratic share in the orientation of an economy dominated
neither by individuals nor by the state, and in which
organized labor will be represented in the management
of industry.

All of these statements of position and declarations
of intention naturally pleased me, and it was enormously
encouraging to find finally coming to the suface such
a widespread support for positions I had long held and
made the basis of my action, but which previously I had
felt obliged to conceal or camouflage. At the same time,
I searched in vain for a change in institutional practice
to correspond to the change in declared principles. Some
of the United States bishops and their advisers were living
like plutocrats and riding around in enormous automobiles
made available to them by powerful United States interests. When the victims of international imperialism urged
the Council to denounce the squandering of billions of
dollars each year on instruments of mass destruction,
some American bishops rallied to the defense of the Pentagon and of United States manufacturers and suppliers
of armaments.

Of course it wasn't just the United States bishops,
although I felt they carried a particular responsibility
because they are the main financial support of the system.
It was the whole Roman system. I always remember
a small incident in St. Peter's during a session of the
Council. I was standing in a corner close to a window.

It was the time they were discussing the birth-control issue, and there had been some very shady maneuvers to prevent the Council from establishing a consensus on an issue which the Curia wanted to dispose of behind the scenes. A man standing beside me identified himself as one of the invited Protestant observers. We got into conversation about the possibilities of ecumenism, and after some sparring, he formulated in the bluntest terms the issue as he saw it. "How, in the name of God, can we start talking to each other until the Catholic Church first becomes honest? I don't say we Protestants are guiltless, but the lead has to be taken by the big Church, and so far, I see no sign of it."

I could not disagree with him, nor can I today. Ever since the Council, the Church has been trying to have the best of both worlds, to hold on to the aristocracy, to the Establishment, and big business, while mouthing nice words to create an appearance of concern for the lower echelons. I saw it once again when I was invited back to Rome in September 1970 to participate in a discussion of the credit union movement under Vatican auspices, sponsored and financed mainly by United States organizations, CUNA, Catholic Relief Services, National Catholic Rural Life Conference, and the National Council of Churches. We are still in the same process of manipulation of people, dirty politics, and schemes of domination deceitfully labeled as service.

To get back to Rome during the Council, my visit for the third session in 1964 served mainly to renew and enlarge my contacts with Latin American bishops. It was the ideal place to reach them. At Domus Mariae alone there were over a hundred Brazilian bishops. Those I got to know best were Eugenio Sales of Natal, Angelo Rossi, who had just been promoted to São Paulo from Ribeirão Preto, and Dom Helder Camara, who a little earlier had gone from Rio de Janeiro to Recife. Bishop

Manuel Larraín of Talca, Chile, the energetic and progressive head of CELAM, who was to die tragically in an automobile accident in June 1966, arranged for me to see most of his fellow countrymen. One of the bishops of Ecuador set up a joint meeting with all the bishops of that country. And so on around the hemisphere. My message for all of them was simple. If they would make arrangements to send promising cooperative leaders from their respective countries to my four-month courses in Panama, the only cost to them would be the travel. Each student's living expenses and instruction in Panama would require more than a thousand dollars, but I would assume responsibility for everything. They listened politely, praised the program, promised to see what they could do—and did nothing. Perhaps that is an exaggeration. The fact that so many bishops knew about my work and were favorably disposed to it may have later helped in unidentifiable ways. But not one of them ever put his hand in his pocket to pay for a round-trip ticket for a single student. Of course, some were so poor themselves that even an air fare would have been a big sacrifice.

ICI Gets Permanent Quarters

In spite of so many disappointments, the success of the 1964 course in Panama encouraged me to try again in 1965, especially as my friends in the United States had given me another $20,000 to underwrite the costs. After a series of adventures and experiences in the United States, including an hour-long appearance on CBS television on a show discussing world poverty, in which Jawaharlal Nehru's daughter, Indira Gandhi, who was shortly to become India's prime minister, was a fellow guest, I got back to Panama on Februrary 11. My arrival had been delayed by a twelve-day stay in a hospital in

Chicago for treatment of an old sacroiliac complaint that suddenly flared up. I was almost helpless, supported by a brace and scarcely able to walk as we scrambled feverishly to get everything ready for the course due to open Februrary 17. Indeed I would have had to call it off at the last moment were it not for the magnificent efforts of a Panamanian lady, Doña Peggy Janson. It was she who found a suitable place to rent, organized the assembly of kitchen, dining room, and dormitory equipment and furnishings, and even found us a cook.

I was still without a place of my own, and the promised aid from the Panamanian government had so far not materialized. Of course, the government was having its own problems. Although the conflict with the United States had been deescalated and diplomatic relations between the two countries renewed, one was always conscious of volcanic rumblings. Just after I got back, a man was murdered one night on the street a stone's throw from the Christian Brothers school which we were using for the first two months of this course. And from our slight elevation, we could look down over the city at night and watch the fires set by arsonists.

Another important detail that had not worked out as I anticipated was the choice of the successor to Archbishop Francis Beckmann of Panama City, who had died at the end of 1963. The odds seemed to favor Mark McGrath, who had been his assistant since 1961 and who had made quite a name for himself at the Vatican Council both for his work in various committees and for his liaison functions between Latin American and North American bishops. Born in Panama of a United States father and Costa Rican mother, and educated both in Panama and in the United States, Mark knew how to behave in both camps. He was also one of the few Latin American bishops who had shown serious interest in the cooperative movement, and his encouragement and promise of help had played a significant part in my decision to take a chance in Panama without first making sure of resources to maintain the work. He did not get the Panama City appointment at that time, however. It went instead to Bishop Thomas Clavel, head of the diocese of David, and Mark was shunted off to the newly created diocese of Santiago in Veraguas Province. He did, however, continue to express an interest. In fact, he wanted me to set up my institute permanently in Santiago rather than in Panama City, and I went so far as to move the students there for the last month of the 1965 course and for the whole of the following year's course. But the idea simply was not feasible. The living facilities were wholly inadequate. Then there was the problem of the professors. To cover all the subjects in the course called for at least a dozen, and ten of those who were available taught in the national university in Panama City, which was a 300-mile round trip. Most of the things we needed were not available locally and communications with the capital were terrible. Even a phone call often took hours. To top it all, once during the dry season the water supply failed and we had to go for three weeks in the intense heat without a shower.

The end result of all of this was a decision to write off Panama and look for another location. I had devoted three years to the experiment and given three courses, one each year. They had been successful up to a point. They had confirmed my belief· that an institute of this kind could make a significant contribution to the development of Latin America. But it was not possible to continue indefinitely on a hand-to-mouth basis. Everything still depended on me personally, the obtaining of funds, the supervision of the courses, the physical presence to be able to step in each day and teach a class in a different subject when a professor failed to turn up. There was no future along those lines.

I traveled to the United States in June 1966, feeling deeply depressed. Friends in the Dominican Republic wanted me to go back there later in the year to give a two-month course for which they hoped to obtain funds from the United States foreign aid program. There were also inquiries for courses from other Latin American countries, something that might keep the idea of the Inter-American Cooperative Institute alive a little longer, but which offered no serious promise of resolving its problems. There was no end of promises and suggestions, but I was getting tired of chasing will-o'-the-wisps. Just to please my friends, nevertheless, I went once again to Washington to see if the foreign aid people could be persuaded to supply the required funding for a permanent center. After another series of meetings and conferences, I came out once more empty-handed.

There was a gloom hanging over Washington, a premonition of what in the following years would be the national nightmare. Nobody at the top levels of government was interested any longer in the Alliance for Progress and all the rest of the bold rhetoric about building a continental partnership to which all the nations of America would devote their united efforts. Instead, concern was being centered on Vietnam, and if you wanted funding, what you had to do was to walk in with a proposal calculated to entrap the United States a little deeper in the quagmire of Southeast Asia.

The money for the short course in the Dominican Republic, $15,000 for forty students for a period of fifty days, was already in the pipeline, and in any case there still was AID money available for that country because of the occupation by the marines the previous year. So that course went off as planned, and when it was ending I was summoned home in the middle of December when my father suffered a heart attack. Fortunately, he rallied quickly, and I decided to spend Christmas with friends in New York and try to figure out what should be my next step. And then, quite unexpectedly, two days before Christmas I received a cable from the Minister of Agriculture of Panama, Rubén D. Carles. He had heard that I was planning to abandon Panama, and he said he himself would help to get me a permanent location and building if I would stay. A second cable and a letter ten days later convinced me that he really meant it. I decided to try once more.

Dr. Carles was indeed serious, so much so that when I arrived in Panama on January 15, he wanted me to repeat the experience of the previous years and improvise yet another course. But by now I saw clearly that such improvisations were endangering the project, and I said the first priority was a permanent home. We started to explore sites and discuss terms, and the negotiations dragged on for two months without getting very far. Then, one day I was at the agriculture ministry, and Phyllis Fong, who was the minister's secretary, introduced me to a man who happened to walk in. His name was Eddy Vallarino, a big businessman and owner of an airline. "What are you doing here, Father?" he asked me. "I'm trying to get a place to operate," I said. "What kind of operation?" I told him. "And how far have you got?" I said I was looking at a piece of land outside the city, but it was costly, and I'd prefer something not so far away. "No problem," he said. "I'll get it for you." Nobody thought he was serious. Even Dr. Carles, the agriculture minister, told me not to waste my time. "You're crazy, Father," he said, "if you think any of the *rabiblancos* is going to give you anything for a program to help the poor." The *rabiblanco* is a white-tailed bird, and its name is given in ridicule to the oligarchs of Panama, who are also known as the *Veinte Familias* (twenty families). But Eddy was as good as his word. For five weeks he was with me every day, rushing around the city, in and out of lawyers' offices. And at the end of that time, all was set for me to take possession of a site that was just right for my purposes. The land was owned by a company headed by a man whose family name was the same as Eddy's, a Mr. J. J. Vallarino. He also became enthusiastic about the project and persuaded his business associates to join him in donating the land. Thanks to its excellent location and the steady growth of the city, it is now worth a quarter million dollars. Doña Margarita Vallarino, Eddy's mother, and Doña Peggy Janson worked with me for weeks soliciting donations from industry and business. Their efforts brought in building materials and furniture to the value of some $35,000. Eddy similarly continued his interest. He helped to get ICI incorporated as an independent nonprofit entity, thus ensuring its independence of both church and state. He is today chairman of the board of ICI. During the eight months that the work was in progress I lived with the Vincentian Fathers. They had been generous hosts in China thirty years ago when I was on the run from the Japanese, and I found exactly the same spirit when I turned to them in Panama.

The rest of 1967 was spent in building and organizing. We worked day and night on the preparation of the site, the construction and the furnishing. When we were finished, we had live-in facilities for sixty-five people, students, teachers, and administrative and supervisory staff, with classrooms, a library, a kitchen, dining room, offices, and dormitories. Then we started to send out brochures to interested parties all over Latin America, because we had decided to open up the facilities to the entire hemisphere. We notified departments of agriculture, federations of cooperatives and credit unions, government-sponsored institutions to promote the cooperative movement and leaders of both the Catholic and Protestant churches. In that first mailing after the building of the permanent facilities, we sent a brochure to each of seven hundred Latin American Catholic bishops and did not get a reply from one of them. In subsequent years, a few have sent students, but it is an uphill fight trying to get any of them—with very few exceptions indeed—to take advantage of the opportunities available in the socioeconomic field. As an indication of clerical attitudes, we have even found it necessary to be particularly careful about accepting priests as students. Some of them want to be accorded special privileges. Instead of agreeing to participate on a level of equality in student activities, such as a student council, for example, they want to be advisers, to the disgust of the other students. I have heard of similar conflicts in Antigonish, Cuernavaca, and Ponce.

The basic structure and content of the course had been worked out over the preceding years, and with permanent quarters it was possible to streamline and perfect it. I had started with the Antigonish program used at the Coady Institute, which has two characteristics: motivation and hope for the poor; and adult education as an integral part of the economic processes of credit unions and other cooperatives. One can find bigger cooperatives in other parts of the world than those of Nova Scotia, and possibly better management, but the human features make the Antigonish variety special, and my experience convinces me that they give it particular value for the developing countries where the primary need is the formation of men and women who believe in themselves and in their ability to create their own future. "The common man is capable," as Father Coady affirmed so vehemently. "We confidently and categorically affirm that the solution of the ills of present-day society is to be found in improvement in the quality of human beings

themselves . . . the regenerated masses will be the force
that will not only bring life to themselves, but also will
be the counterforce that will knock down the mighty from
their seats of power and re-establish that balance and
equilibrium which have so seriously been interfered with
in recent times . . . That is the plain logic of the situation."

The Antigonish approach to education differs sharply
from the conventional one which isolates students in a
teacher-pupil relationship for years, until they finally
emerge with a piece of paper and a conviction that they
have learned all they will ever need to know about the
subjects they studied. Of course, the contemporary explosion of knowledge is making clear to everyone that this
method was based on a fallacy. But the Antigonish
approach starts from a different philosophical premise.
Its principle is that education must be social, and this
is a principle with which Paulo Freire, the Brazilian
educator, agrees when he describes education as a process. He says that it is not really correct to say "I think,"
but always that "we think," meaning that the very act
of thinking is a social one. He criticizes the traditional
system of "pouring in" knowledge into the heads of learn-
ers, an approach still common in schools in Latin
America, where learning by rote is regarded more highly
than thinking for oneself. Since learning is a process,
he says, there must be a two-way dialogue of teacher
and student. The Antigonish pioneers popularized this
kind of dialogue in their study circles and kitchen meetings, and it is integral to the ICI courses. The "pouring
in" of facts has its role to play in learning, because you
can't have knowledge unless it is a knowledge of something. But education is more than the acquiring of facts.
It is not static. Rather, it is an activity of the mind.
The mind is applied to facts to understand them, digest
them, and apply them to life.

A related aspect of the Antigonish approach which we also practice at ICI is what I may call the economy of education. We do not try to impart all knowledge in a single dose, but only the knowledge needed to perform at a certain level. As my friend and mentor, Father Jimmy Tompkins of Antigonish, used to say: "The time for learning anything is when you need it . . . " Later, when the first injection has been fully assimilated, those who need further knowledge to perform higher tasks can come back for additional courses, until gradually each one finds the level at which he has the greatest contribution to make.

Perhaps the place where this approach has been applied most widely and systematically is Denmark, as I was able to see for myself on a recent visit. Denmark's folk high schools, which I consider admirably suited for Latin America, were started in the middle of the last century by a clergyman-poet, Nikolai F. S. Grundtvig, and their purpose was to stimulate the intellectual life of young adults between the ages of fifteen and twenty-four. They concentrated on the "national and community life we all can and must share in." Grundtvig's initiative was taken up by Christen Kold,who spread it throughout the country, especially in the rural areas. The schools set out not just to impart knowledge but to stir interest in human problems and encourage dialogue. Their students were the principal initiators and spreaders of the cooperative movement in Denmark in the last century. They also established democratic politics and played a major role in reforming the official Lutheran Church. The folk schools have neither entrance nor final examinations. Students arrange their own syllabus from a curriculum which usually includes the Danish language, religion, mathematics, civics, history, and psychology. In addition to listening to lectures, the students participate actively in study circles and other group activities, all of which stress character formation. Courses run from a few weeks to six months, some for men only, others for women only, and yet others for both sexes. The schools are administered privately, but are subsidized by the state.

The basic course for cooperative leaders at Antigonish runs for eight months, being geared to coincide with and fit into the academic year of the university. Not only for reasons of cost but because many of the potential students of ICI would already be working either in cooperatives or agricultural extension and could not afford to be away so long, we decided to cover the same ground in an intensive course of four months. It is a tremendous scramble both for students and professors. We work every day from early morning until late at night. But the students are highly motivated, and there are advantages from maintaining an intense rhythm rather than the measured pace of university life.

The student or some sponsoring agency on his behalf must pay travel costs to and from Panama. ICI houses and teaches him free. All we insist on is that he have a high-school certificate or equivalent educational background, and also an assurance that he will be employed full-time in the socioeconomic field on his return home. Most such jobs are in government employment or in organizations sponsored by governments, the typical jobs being promoters of cooperatives or credit unions, agricultural extension agents and community development leaders. In addition, the cooperative movement itself provides many openings as it develops, organizers of new cooperatives, federation officials, store managers, and so on. Professional people also find the courses of benefit to them. In fact, some 20 percent of the students are agronomists, engineers, architects, lawyers, social workers, or other professionals.

In broad terms, the course devotes four weeks to management and business administration, two weeks to credit unions, six weeks to all the other kinds of cooperatives,

and three weeks to motivation, leadership, and ethical
formation. All of this adds up to more than five hundred
hours of classroom theory and three weeks of field work.
The specific subjects taught are bookkeeping, cooperatives and credit unions, community development and land
reform, management and business administration, group
dynamics and sensitivity training, sociology and political
science, basic notions of agriculture, public speaking,
legislation, and adult education. The field work is conducted in rural Panama, in Antioquia, Colombia, or in
one òf the neighboring countries of Central America.
Students observe and evaluate the working of existing
cooperatives, consumer, fisheries, marketing, and so on.
They participate in meetings of the members of credit
unions and cooperatives and engage in a variety of projects of agricultural extension and community development.

One major addition to the original Antigonish curriculum is the group dynamics and sensitivity, training.
Since most of the students come from remote villages
and have the instinctive peasant resistance to revealing
their inmost thoughts and desires in public, a way has
to be found to get them out of themselves if they are
to function efficiently as group leaders. I had long been
conscious of this need, and back in the 1950's when I
was still in the Dominican Republic, I decided to participate in a three-week group dynamics course being held
at a junior college in Bethel, Maine. There were about
150 of us, mostly college professors, some business
executives, a fair number of Protestant ministers. I was
the only Catholic priest. They told me there had only
been one before me, a Jesuit. They broke us into groups
of fourteen, called T-groups ("T" for training), each
under a moderator. Our moderator was a stone-faced
Englishman. We sat around a table for three 3-hour sessions each day, without any program. After a while, some-

one broke the silence and asked what was the crazy idea. Then, an hour later, someone else said this was a very expensive way to waste his time and if something didn't happen soon, he would take off for home. Then someone else began to attack the moderator who maintained his stone-faced silence. People fought and bickered, reacted to each other, revealed their prejudices, their fears, their emotional hangups. From time to time, the moderator intervened to describe what each person had said and done. He made no evaluation, simply recalling each incident and allowing the actors to figure out the meaning for themselves. The process was hard on the nerves but fascinating. By the time it finished, I thought it was one of the most valuable experiences ever, and it left me with a whole series of techniques to be used in the training of leaders. I applied it as best I could on my own in subsequent training courses in the Dominican Republic and in Panama, not having the resources then to hire a professional team. But ever since we got our own ICI building, the experiment has been done properly.

For the first course, in 1967, I brought two qualified group dynamics leaders from Puerto Rico, a doctor and a psychiatrist. Next time I got three Guatemalans, headed by a psychiatrist. By then, a team of Panamanians has been developed, and that makes it possible to split the course in group dynamics into two parts, five days at the beginning of the term and two at the end. Nowadays, a T-trainer will take a maximum of ten students, which means that we need a team of three for the average class of thirty. What I find fascinating is the response of the students themselves. We hold a jamboree at the end of each term, and the students get up in turn to give their own evaluation of the course. Almost without exception, they stress the benefit of the group dynamics, and the comments vary little from one class to another. Many stress their ability for the first time to recognize their

own defects. "I've learned how false I've been . . . I
realized how unsocial I was . . . It never occurred to
me before that I was consistently cruel to my wife . . . "
Another stress is a new awareness of the way others
look at one, an understanding of personality factors which
prevent people from liking him, or which make it hard
for him to get along with others, "I am beginning to
understand what happens when people work in groups,
why groups break up, why they fail to work out their
frictions . . . I am now able to listen to a question and
make an attempt to understand what is behind it, instead
of going off halfcocked when somebody interrupts . . .
I am more sincere both with myself and with the people
around me . . . "

Another leadership training technique with which we
have begun to experiment is closed-circuit television. A
relatively simple unit, of which the heart is a video-tape
recorder, makes it possible for individuals and groups
to study and evaluate their own performance. When I
visited Scandinavia in 1970, I discovered that this training
tool is widely used and rated highly. Then I learned that
the Michigan credit union league in the United States
was also using it and finding it very helpful. We obtained
the equipment at ICI and we have begun to use it profit-
ably. The operating techniques are not hard to learn,
but it does require one extra person to do the job right,
and each year I promise myself that next year we will
be able to afford him.

Through the end of 1971, some four hundred students
from twenty-three countries had graduated from these
basic courses, and I am happy to say that most of them
are using the specialized knowledge they acquired. Many
are employees of their own governments. Others are
directors, administrators, and teachers in about sixty
private institutions dedicated to the promotion of
cooperative and rural development in all parts of Latin

America. ICI also gives short advanced courses in management, marketing, and the administration of agricultural cooperatives in conjunction with the Organization of Cooperatives of the Americas (OCA) and the governments of Panama and Israel, as well as advanced courses for credit union administrators in conjunction with CUNA's regional office for Latin America. Its facilities are also extensively used for short courses and seminars given by organizations working in development, including various sections of the Panama government and groups associated with both Catholic and Protestant churches. As the cooperative movement grows in Latin America, the need for specialized and advanced training becomes progressively greater. All we have at ICI is just a start, but it is a solid foundation on which a great human edifice can be built.

5

LATIN AMERICA

What the Cooperative Movement Does

I am frequently asked two related questions. What are cooperatives supposed to do for a country? What have cooperatives done for Latin America? These are two enormously important questions, particularly for me. How could I justify having put my life's effort into this movement, and how could I encourage others to become involved with me, unless I had some idea of the goal I am seeking, and unless I had some evidence that I was making reasonable progress toward that goal?

Let me say, first of all, that I am not so naive as to pretend that cooperatives provide a panacea for all the world's ills. Although the movement has been introduced to a greater or lesser extent into every country of Latin America, it has not developed anywhere in this hemisphere to the point of making a significant contribution to the solution of the region's enormous economic and social problems. While recognizing that fact, I am absolutely convinced, as a result of my personal observation and evaluation over a quarter of a century, that it is a technique suited to the objective needs of Latin America. More specifically, I believe that the approach I learned in Antigonish, an approach that emphasizes education and gives cooperatives a social as well as an economic purpose, is the one that offers the greatest hope and promises the highest dividends. It has to be combined with other factors, especially land reform, as I shall explain in a moment. But it is a method that can and must bring hope to millions who previously had no way to improve themselves, hope that they and their children can achieve a decent life as human beings.

More than half a billion people in some seventy countries around the world are members of cooperatives. In Sweden, one of the world's socially most progressive countries, upwards of 90 percent of agriculture, which is the country's only major natural resource, is in the hands of cooperatives; and they also control as much as 50 percent of many industries and a substantial proportion of trade. An important result of this distribution of economic power is that it protects the consumer from monopolistic practices. In the typical Latin American town or village, a handful of merchants frequently control the entire process of buying and selling. They fix their profit margins, decide who gets credit and on what terms, maintain the entire community in a condition of poverty and slavery. Obviously, when people control their own credit resources through credit unions, and do their own buying and selling through their consumer and marketing cooperatives, this stranglehold can no longer be exercised. And with freedom from economic dictation, the conditions for political democracy are also created, a process further encouraged by the democratic procedures which are basic to the functioning of credit unions and cooperatives.

It is true, of course, that the cooperative movement does not create a utopia. People are still people. All over the world, one can find so-called cooperatives in which people have united for selfish ends to enjoy the privileges conferred by law on cooperatives. People who unite merely to promote their own interests constitute a capitalistic corporation, perhaps a cartel. When I was in Sweden, a man who had spent his entire life in the cooperative movement said to me: "Here in Sweden, many of us call the farmers who are in the cooperative movement capitalists, and the urban cooperative people socialists." Since the farmers' cooperatives in Sweden control 90 percent of agricultural activity, there is a danger that they may become a new monopoly and use their power to raise the price to the urban consumer unduly. As far as Latin America is concerned, I think it would be enough to say that the possibility of a similar monopoly is so remote as not to be worth considering. If we could get up to 20 percent from the present level of probably less than 1 percent, we would have enough counterpower to serve as a brake on monopolistic gouging. If two centuries from now, the proportion rises to 50 percent, then maybe it will be time to worry.

There is also another aspect of this issue that should not be ignored. The nature of capitalism is the pursuit of profits. Our capitalist merchants in Latin America are being faithful to the perverted principles of capitalism when they exercise their monopoly to squeeze the poor. But the same is not true of the Swedish farmers to the extent that they may gouge the urban consumers. The principles of the cooperative movement are clear. It insists on justice in exchange, a fair return to the producer, a fair price to the consumer, the elimination of all parasitic traders from the process of getting producer and consumer together. Where the members of a cooperative have been adequately educated in the principles, they will understand the importance of justice in all their dealings. A public opinion against gouging will gradually permeate the entire community. It is when the all-important educational process has been bypassed that distortions occur, and this is particularly evident in government-sponsored programs both in Latin America and elsewhere. Bureaucrats anxious for visible results concentrate on techniques to the exclusion or ignoring of the spirit. The result can only be capitalism disguised under cooperative forms.

In Chapter 3 I described how the cooperative movement grew in the Dominican Republic to the point where some members of the oligarchy saw it as threatening their traditional monopoly of decision making and promising the peasants a significant degree of control over their own destinies, only to be crushed by the traditional holders of power. Elsewhere, the same process has occurred, if less dramatically. In the typical village, power has always been the monopoly of a small group of landowners, merchants, and moneylenders. So far, no cooperative movement has succeeded in escaping from their clutches.

Is there a way to break this vicious circle? Father Moses Coady of Antigonish was convinced that there is, and so am I. "We have to get over the naive idea," Father Coady once said, "that monopolistic exploiters and dictators are going to reform because good men preaching justice and charity tell them to do so. Experience has shown that bad men generally will reform only when they have to. We must, therefore, add force to our persuasion. This does not mean physical force and bloodshed, but it does call for the force of ideas, expressed in terms of a program that will give a legitimate share of power to the people."

The first step in the development of a program is an analysis of the situation which will identify and isolate the monopolistic exploiters of whom Father Coady speaks. What then do we see when we look at the Latin American situation? Perhaps the most important thing is to recognize that it is no longer static, as it was for centuries. Population is close to the 300 million mark and growing rapidly. Although the gross domestic product is also growing at more or less the same rate as the population, the distribution of the benefits of that growth is concentrated in the upper 20 percent of the population, so that the masses become steadily poorer and more frustrated, encouraging the violence that is present almost everywhere.

Another factor that must be taken into account is the subhuman level at which so many people live. Ever since the Spanish Conquest, society has been established not only on a class system but on structures which allowed for the availability at all times of a reserve of surplus labor consisting mainly of the indigenous Indians or of the imported African slaves and their descendants. In both cases, this marginal element had been stripped of its own cultural heritage without any serious effort to provide the alternative culture of the conquerors. Its members have lived and live by their own devices, something like the wild animals that used to roam the prairies. When some are needed to perform work for their masters, they are rounded up for the required purpose, then turned loose again to shift for themselves. My first efforts in the Dominican Republic were with people close to that level. Since they are deficient in the basic human virtues of thrift, of trust, of self-reliance, they are not yet ready to participate in the cooperative movement. An enormous effort to achieve their development as human beings must precede. It is a problem with which many Latin American intellectuals are now wrestling. Of the various experiments so far attempted, the most promising seems to be the educational method of *conscientização* developed by the Brazilian Paulo Freire. Now widely practiced around the continent, it seems to give excellent technical results, although political resistance by the powerful groups who fear the awakening of the masses has prevented any major breakthrough.

Alongside the totally suppressed groups, there is an enormous mass of poor people both in the countryside and in city slums who have acquired enough education and enough cultural integration to be ready for incorporation into the credit union and cooperative movements, people like those in the Cibao of the Dominican Republic who have in the past twenty years significantly improved their living levels and their community organization through cooperatives, in spite of the continual political unrest and violence around them. Their extreme poverty is a factor limiting the rate of advance both in the Dominican Republic and elsewhere in Latin America. For many of them the struggle to live is such that it takes years of heroic effort to build up a capital of a few dollars.

There is, however, no limit to what people can do if they are properly motivated, as I was reminded one evening many years ago while I was participating in a credit union meeting in a small town in the northern part of the Dominican Republic. A member asked me if I agreed with him that many of the people in the town were too poor to become members of the credit union. I said I agreed. Then another member—whom I will call Ernesto—spoke up. "I believe you are both mistaken," he said, "and I will explain why. Nobody in this city is poorer than I was three years ago. I live with one woman with seven children, but I have another eight women in different places, all of them with children. I have never counted the exact number of my offspring. I make frames for pictures, mostly pictures of the saints, and I earn about eight dollars a week on the average. I own nothing except the few tools I use to make the picture frames, and I never owned anything more in my life. But after three years in the credit union, I have saved nearly one hundred dollars by little sacrifices. I

visit my other women less often, and for the past year
I have given up entirely my weekend flask of rum. I
never thought it possible. Now I am purchasing a building
lot and I hope to put up my own house on it next year
and get married to one woman. I am not yet sure which
one of the eight, but I am studying the matter."

Needless to say, the whole hall was in laughter as
Ernesto related the details of his life style with total frank-
ness. Even the daily diet was described. "Not one of
them is skinny, I assure you," he said. "If you don't
believe me, I will bring them here to let you see for
yourself that they are all well fed." Ernesto went ahead
faithfully with his plans and in due course became the
owner of his own home. When I saw him a few years
later, he also owned a small shop, with two hired helpers.
He had his marriage blessed in church; or, as he put
it, "I now own one woman." He was proud of himself,
and with good reason. And I also was proud of him,
as I saw him walk up the aisle in the church with his
fifty-year-old bride of many seasons.

When people become motivated the way Ernesto was
and throw themselves seriously into the credit union and
cooperative movement, the impact on the quality of their
lives is dramatic. In a period as short as five or six years,
they can double their living standards. But they still have
a long way to go. At this point the existing power structures become conscious of the threat to their monopoly
of economic and political decision-making. At first, while
the peasants are gathering in small groups in a little shack
to talk, especially if the program is sponsored by the
local priest, nobody is concerned. But when the credit
union becomes a source of credit at a fraction of the
rates charged by the money-lenders, when the consumer
cooperative sells corn during the scarce period at a fifth
of the price charged by the merchants, the reaction
develops rapidly and massively.

Magazine articles and books written by economists and social scientists for publication in the United States frequently are eloquent in their descriptions of the progress made in one Latin American country after another by cooperatives recently established and still in their first stages of development. It is clear, they argue, that we can create a dynamic economy in which every citizen will have access to the good life by a more intensive application of adult education, trade unions, community development, and cooperatives. Time and again this projection has been proved unrealistic and utopian. What actually happens is that the holders of power turn to illegal methods when necessary in order to destroy the development that threatens them. This new stage of institutionalized violence to protect the rich against the poor is taking the form of vigilante movements in country after country. In one of the most sinister of recent developments in Latin America, these groups of thugs roam the countryside and terrorize all incipient popular leaders. They have long been a feature of life in Guatemala, where they are known as *La Mano* (the hand) or *Ojo por Ojo* (an eye for an eye), and in Brazil, where they are called *Squadrones da Morte* (death squads). More recently, they have started in the Dominican Republic as *La Banda* (the band) and in Mexico as *Los Halcones* (the falcons). The impunity with which they operate in tight police states is an indication of the level of official complicity. Their ability to supply themselves with modern arms and to pay their members handsomely causes many to suspect CIA subsidization.

Land Reform Is an Essential Step

We recently had here in Panama an example of the multiple difficulties encountered by a program designed to create an area of rural well-being within a traditional Latin

American society. An ambitious program of development was drawn up in the mid-1960's in the province of Veraguas in western Panama, under church auspices. Known as the Veraguas Plan, it included elements of adult education, community development, and cooperatives. This program was studied in detail by a group of economists and social scientists headed by George C. Lodge, a professor at the Harvard Business School and formerly an assistant secretary for international affairs of the United States Department of Labor. In a book published in 1969, *Engines of Change,* Lodge cited Veraguas in support of his thesis that the traditional power structures would not be able to prevent the creation of new bases of power among the peasants through cooperatives, unionization, and political education. Within two years of the publication of the Lodge book, however, it had become clear that the scenario it presented was unduly simplistic and optimistic. The Veraguas Plan has had only token and marginal impact on the economy and the society, and the enthusiasm it generated at first is largely dissipated because of the ability of the holders of power to negate each serious effort to shake off the traditional controls.

The Lodge thesis, according to which the poor countries of the world can create acceptable living levels for all their people through cooperatives and other "technical" devices without any radical change of structures, is interesting mainly because it has been the official position of the United States government since the death of John F. Kennedy. At Punta del Este, Uruguay, in 1961, President Kennedy committed the United States by treaty in the Alliance for Progress to give top priority to a radical land reform in Latin America. One of the primary goals of the Alliance was "to encourage . . . programs of comprehensive agrarian reform, leading to the effective transformation, where required, of unjust structures and systems of land tenure and use, with a view to replacing latifundia and dwarf holdings by an equitable system of property so that . . . the land will become for the man who works it the basis of his economic stability, the foundation of his increasing welfare, and the guarantee of his freedom and dignity."

The big landlords, for whom land is not only wealth but also power, naturally resisted. Simultaneously, the United States policy makers became frightened by the enormous popular forces unleashed by the first tentative steps in various countries to implement the commitment. The local oligarchs in one country after another had little difficulty in persuading them that any change in the rural power structure would open the way to new Cubas. They accordingly agreed to give Alliance aid without waiting for the promised land reform. At most, token action was taken for the record. Various countries gave titles to squatters who were already in effective occupation of government land. They proposed grandiose schemes to open up"virgin territories." But they always stopped short of disturbing the power structure.

Seven years after the promulgation of the Charter of Punta del Este, the Economic Commission for Latin America of the United Nations issued a report documenting the failure of the promised land reforms. It said that none of the "realistic targets" for land reform set by the Alliance for Progress had been met. Instead, "the Latin American countries have achieved very little in absolute terms and practically nothing in relation to the needs . . . Although the enactment of land reform legislation and the establishment of land reform institutes were expected to signal the beginning of a new era of profound changes in the structure of land tenure, in fact most of the reform programs have constantly been watered down and many of them are almost at a standstill. . . . The

number of families settled thus far is only a fraction of
the annual natural increase in farm families. . . . In other
words, thus far land reform activities have made only
a very small dent in the land tenure system, and none
of the programs have reached the proportions of a real
land reform."

As a concrete confirmation of these general conclusions, I may cite some figures from a study made in
1970 by the faculty of economic and social sciences of
the Autonomous University of Santo Domingo. In 1960,
almost 45 percent of the agricultural land of the Dominican Republic was held by less than 1 percent of farmers,
while at the other end of the scale, 310,340 families lived
on uneconomical micro-holdings. Ten years later, the
proportion of land held by big landowners was unchanged.
The Land Reform Institute had given family farms to 7,068
peasants, while the number of micro-holdings had
increased as a result of population pressures to 450,000
with a corresponding decrease in the average size.

The experience of other Latin American countries was
similar. Even President Eduardo Frei of Chile, the Christian Democrat who promised a revolution in freedom
when elected in 1964, created only 15,000 units during
his six-year term instead of the 100,000 he had promised.
His program had grounded to a halt long before the term
ended, as the government tried to keep peace between
peasants frustrated by delays and landlords organized
to hold on to all their productive properties. It is certainly
noteworthy that the only major land reforms in Latin
America have been in Mexico, Bolivia, and Cuba, in
all three by violent revolution and over the opposition
of the United States. This fact must be kept in mind
when reflecting on the decision of the Chileans, people
noted in Latin America for their commitment to the
democratic process and for their freedom from civil strife

and military takeovers, to choose a prominent Marxist, Salvádor Allende, as president in 1970. They had seen the frustration of all efforts at reform during the Frei presidency by an alliance of Rightists and Leftists, and this apparently made them willing to risk the loss of their civil liberties in a regime that could evolve into communism. It is clear that many Latin Americans have lost faith in the only kind of democracy they have known, and also in the dictatorial regimes under which they have suffered. The only alternatives left seem to be the socialism the Chileans are now trying and the state capitalism that goes by the name of communism.

I was particularly impressed by the high priority accorded to land reform by Gunnar Myrdal, the Swedish economist and sociologist, in his book, *The Challenge of World Poverty*, (New York, Pantheon, 1970). Dr. Myrdal's international reputation goes back to a pioneer study of race in the United States which was published in the early 1940's. After that came studies of development in Asia, particularly in the Indian subcontinent. Now for the first time he devotes major attention to Latin America, and always with the same keen insights. Speaking of the Alliance for Progress, he comments that the reforms it proposed, including land reform, were "rapidly emasculated by interaction between the holders of power in Latin America, including the American corporations working there, and the United States government and Congress." He also warns that the substitutes for true reform currently promoted and financed by the United States, including the so-called miracle seeds, will not achieve their objectives and will instead increase the distortions as long as the first essential for human development—land reform—is bypassed. The reason for this is that the benefits of the miracle seeds are available only to the big operator who uses fertilizers, insecticides, irrigation, and machinery. The peasants become more marginal than before.

The decision of the rich countries to abandon the efforts they were making ten or fifteen years ago to promote social reform in the poor countries is regarded by Dr. Myrdal as a betrayal. It is "a gross misjudgment of facts and betrayal of ideals on the part of Western nations and, in the first instance, by the United States." He blames the change on the manipulation of public opinion by opportunists motivated by their own interests, often petty and short-term. "The goal of the developed countries and, in particular, the United States has not been that the masses should be awakened in order to make possible genuine democracy and the radical reforms needed. All their sympathies were with the privileged classes in the underdeveloped countries and not with the impoverished masses. They were readily prepared to con- done the absence of reforms in underdeveloped countries, or the perversion of reforms, preferring stability—in fact, a sort of continuation of colonial practices."

Again and again Dr. Myrdal returns to the primacy of land reform. "In most underdeveloped coun- tries . . . land reform has been a sham," he writes. "The spread of the use of the new seed grains, as of other improved techniques, will not reach far without an agrarian reform. Indeed, without such reform, the availability of the new seed grains will join the other forces of reaction that are now tending to increase inequal- ity." There is no way to bypass a land reform which will create "such a relationship between man and the land" as to "make possible and create the incentive for the tiller to work more, work harder and more effectively, to invest whatever funds he can lay his hands on for raising yields and improving his land, and in the first place to invest his own labor for these purposes."

Dr. Myrdal's reference to manipulations by the United States to promote its own interests, often petty and short-term, brings me to a difficult point in my evaluation of the Latin American scene. Like most Canadians, I have always had ambivalent attitudes toward my neighbors. A look at the map will show that Boston is the major city nearest to Nova Scotia as the crow flies, and the most accessible. Many Nova Scotians emigrated there in search of work, and there were frequent comings and goings for business or health reasons. My first extended stay in the United States was when I went to St. Vincent's Hospital in New York for an intensive course in first aid and the rudiments of medicine and surgery before setting out for China. The Americans I then met were without exception overwhelmingly generous and helpful. I learned how to pull teeth and set broken bones. I assisted at operations and gave the anesthetic. I went out on the ambulance on calls. Later, when I became a chaplain to the American troops in Southwest China, I thought they were the greatest people in the world, kind, generous, with a good sense of humor.

Always, nevertheless, there was another side. The Nova Scotians who came back after working in New England described the people there as braggards and superficial, and I could also see those traits in the Americans with whom I associated in China. That applied to the priests as well as the troops. I remember the discussions we used to have in the house where I lived in Chungking. We would be listening to the war news, and Father Edward McManus, the Irish Columban Father, used to get furious at the reactions of the Americans. For people from a big country, they were incredibly insular, talking as if nobody but themselves was doing anything in the war. Their ignorance of the rest of the world was colossal.

But that was a detail which I quickly shook off and

put out of my mind. When I went to the Dominican Republic after returning from China, I was surprised to find such widespread antipathy to the United States, and at that time I felt much of it was not justified. Subsequently, when I spent most of my time for several years in the United States in the early 1960's, I found myself being dragged apart more than ever. On the one side, there was much generosity and hospitality. Indeed, as I have mentioned several times, my main financial support for establishing the Inter-American Cooperative Institute in Panama came from friends in the United States, as does the continuing support to maintain it. On the other hand, government organizations, public foundations, and the churches are heavily institutionalized and bureaucratized. It was not enough to show that a particular course of action was right and deserved support. To win approval from all parties, it was usually necessary to convince each of them that he would also gain something as a result.

Perhaps the turning point in my evaluation of the United States was the long trip I made all through Latin America in late 1962 and early 1963. There I became conscious of the widespread and growing disillusionment of Latin Americans with the United States and put it into a better perspective. The leaders of the movements of Christian inspiration were openly joining the Marxists in rejecting the entire concept of development which underlay the Alliance for Progress and the other programs being offered by the rich countries. Such programs were not working and would not work, they insisted. The facts are beyond question. Each year the gap between the rich countries and the poor ones grows wider. Each year, also, the gap between the small upper group and the impoverished masses in the poor countries grows similarly wider. The obvious conclusion is that the rich countries are not trying to improve the conditions of the poor ones. Rather, they are exploiting the poor for their own selfish benefit.

The more the record is studied, the more reasonable this conclusion appears. It is a fact, for example, that foreign capital, most of it from the United States, controls the exploitation of some 90 percent of the mineral assets of Latin America. United States companies also own and exploit much land devoted to the production of the luxury products of agriculture. It is the biggest purchaser of the region's sugar, coffee, cacao, copper, tin, and petroleum. Prices are set and decisions affecting the livelihood of the workers and the development of the local economy are made in New York, not in Caracas or Rio de Janeiro. United States direct investment grew from $8 billion to $15 billion during the 1960's and it continues to grow at the rate of a billion dollars a year. And during that period, the profits sent back to the United States were more than twice as much as the new investments.

Other forms of control are added to the economic. There is, for example, a high degree of political interference. Cable and telephone communications are for the most part operated by United States companies, permitting the monitoring of messages by agents of the United States. The embassies maintain staffs among whose functions it is to collect information about the activities of individuals and groups regarded by the Pentagon, the State Department, or the CIA as potentially inimical to United States interests. University professors purportedly engaged on scientific investigations and even a few United States citizens serving the Catholic Church have proved to be part of the espionage apparatus. Hundreds of future leaders from nearly every country of Latin America are trained in the Military School of the Americas in the Panama Canal Zone, and graduates of this school are today in top posts in several of the military dictatorships which flourish throughout Latin America with United States approval or connivance. Nor does the United States hesitate to send its own marines to invade Latin American countries and impose its solution for their problems. The most recent such action was the already mentioned invasion of the Dominican Republic in 1965.

The industrial and commercial life of the region is also controlled in large part by United States capital. Everywhere in the business sectors of the cities one can observe the impact of United States advertising, ranging from advertisements for Coca Cola to women's dress and hair styles. Hollywood's movies simultaneously make profits at the box office and condition minds. Even the thousands of priests, brothers, and nuns working as Catholic missionaries unwittingly contribute to the spread of United States culture. Of the hundreds of missionaries from the United States whom I know personally, and many of whom I count as close and sincere friends, only a very small minority could be said to put religion before their homeland in their scale of values. Only in the rarest cases do they succeed in escaping from the chauvinism that is an intimate element in their culture.

This paternalism of North Americans strengthens the negative aspects of the Spanish colonial heritage. The rule of the Spaniards in Latin America was always personalistic. The boss was the *patrón*. He distributed patronage, both in his dealings with his own employees and in his dealings with the public when he held public office. Everyone took it for granted that he should manipulate both private and public affairs for his own benefit. And he in turn accepted the inevitability of arbitrary decisions affecting his own life made in far-off Madrid by people who lacked understanding of his problems. It all added up to a sense of inferiority, which inevitably led to bitterness and hatred. Now Madrid has been replaced by New York, but the rest of the scenario seems little changed to the average Latin American. He continues to lack any effective voice in the processes which determine his destiny.

Christianity and Marxism

In addition to the controls exercised by the United States, the countries of Latin America are burdened by their own wealthy classes, the oligarchs and politicians who rule them. Capitalism in Latin America is still mostly of the nineteenth-century variety, with vestiges of feudalism. Unlike the United States, where the rule is high turnover and low profit margins, Latin American capitalists believe in big profits and low turnover. They avoid risk-taking, preferring to stash away millions of dollars in United States and Swiss banks. In fairness, it should be noted at the same time that the problem of capital flight is a complicated one. Political instability is often a factor. In addition, local capital sometimes finds itself unable to compete with the international companies who enjoy greater access to technology and easier credit. It then has no choice but to go abroad to be lent in the world money market and return under the contol of the international conglomerates.

It is a fact of history that religion has always been at the service of the power structures of Latin America, helping to create and maintain the mentality of resignation and passivity characteristic of the poor. In this respect, the role of religion in Latin America has been quite different from its role in North America. Arnold Toynbee and other historians have pointed out that modern civilization began with the break away from the medieval disciplines in the last quarter of the fifteenth century. Up to that time, the Catholic Church not only controlled the consciences of the people but also held vast political and economic power. The modern world was a product of the Protestant Reformation. The new freedoms it introduced coincided with the discovery of the New World and with the opening up of mental horizons to the possibility of even more worlds to discover and conquer. The earth was finally established to be round and not flat. Scientists, bankers, and inventors were all filled with new enthusiasms. Men ceased to be awed by nature or tied down by old superstitions. They became determined to become their own masters.

The Protestant ethos which grew out of the Reformation is regarded by most historians and sociologists as having played a significant part in developing the drive of the early Americans to conquer the wilderness and build a great nation. While John Calvin's role is the subject of some differences of opinion, the prevailing view is that his philosophy was more influential than that of any other religious leader. He insisted that man should be responsible, that he should rely on himself, work hard, be honest, be a good citizen and neighbor. Work was for him the great virtue. God blesses those who work and ensures that they will prosper. Whatever Calvin's original intentions might have been, in practice his teaching was understood as making success the test of virtue. The prosperous businessman was automatically judged a holy man and blessed by God. It was a philosophy that fitted perfectly with the capitalist system, matching many of Adam Smith's economic theories. Such was the attitude of the Protestants who dominated the settlement of North America and who gave it an outlook and a culture that have survived right down to modern times.

Latin America had no experience with this Protestant ethos during its formative period, and even today it is little influenced by it. Catholicism was the state religion in Spanish and Portuguese times, and it still remains the state religion for all practical purposes in most countries. It is a socially conditioned form of Roman Catholicism, deriving from the medieval Catholicism of southern Europe, very different from the Catholicism of contemporary Germany or Holland. At the popular level, it centered on a series of preoccupations, such as death, health, and immediate temporal concerns. This preoccupation in turn gave rise to a number of practices, prayer to favorite saints, sprinkling of holy water, a system of promises or commitments to perform certain actions or abstain from certain actions in return for a favor one sought from God. While on the one hand the Christianity preached by the Spaniards freed the Indian spiritually by its stress on God's love and mercy, it tended simultaneously on the other hand to compound his traditional fear of nature by introducing new supernatural terrors. God joined nature as an inscrutable and seemingly arbitrary judge of man's fate, a God who was in practice controlled by the Church in his decision and who told the individual through the Church what he should do and not do. Eternal salvation was singled out as the one important thing, with this life no more than a time of waiting and watching. Religious teaching stressed the importance of the sacraments as dispensed by the Church in its graciousness. It spoke of supernatural virtues which were gifts of God and devoted little attention to the natural virtues necessary to achieve development. In contrast to the Calvinist creed which proclaimd that wealth was a mark of God's favor, this philosophy preached that God loved the poor, failing to make the distinction that God loves a man not because he is poor or rich, but because and to the extent that he is good.

Karl Marx said that religion is the opium of the people, and I think that few today would have difficulty in agreeing with his negative evaluation of the kind of religion I have just described, the religion commonly found in Latin America which urges the poor to be resigned to their poverty as being the will of God.

The Catholic Church has officially repudiated this kind of religion. As the Second Vatican Council expressed it in the opening words of its magnificent statement on the Church in the modern world, "The joys and the hopes, the griefs and the anxieties of the men of this age, especially those who are poor or in any way afflicted, these too are the joys and hopes, the griefs and anxieties of the followers of Christ." This general statement of position was taken up and applied to its own situation by the Catholic Church in Latin America when its bishops came together in Colombia in September 1968, in a hemispheric assembly opened by Pope Paul VI in person. The outcome of that meeting was the publication of the Medellín documents as an expression of the consensus of the bishops on the religious, social, economic, and political condition of Latin America.

These documents constitute a 40,000-word call to basic reform, offering the concept of a liberating God to replace the god of private property. They denounce the oppressing power used by institutions to impose violence, the neocolonialism of the national oligarchies, and the external neocolonialism of the "international monopolies and the international imperialism of money," on which the system rests. They specifically list some of the worst effects of all this: the growing distortion of international commerce caused by a decline in the prices of raw materials while those of manufactured goods rise, the flight of capital, the brain drain, the growing burden of debt, tax evasion, and the export of profits and dividends by foreign companies "without contributing the adequate reinvestments to the progressive development of our countries."

According to the Latin American bishops the situation is indeed critical:

> Many parts of Latin America are experiencing a situation of injustice which can be called institutionalized violence. The structures of industry and agriculture, the national and international economy, the cultural and political life all violate fundamental rights. Entire peoples lack the bare necessities and live in a condition of such dependency that they can exercise neither initiative nor responsibility. Similarly, they lack all possibility of cultural improvement and of participation in social and political life. Such situations call for global, daring and basically renewing change. It should surprise nobody that the temptation to violence should manifest itself in Latin America. It is wrong to abuse the patience of people who have endured for years a situation that would be intolerable if they were more aware of their rights as human beings.

These powerful statements were issued at Medellín as the collective voice of all the bishops of Latin America. Subsequently, the bishops in most of the countries have published their own statements, reaffirming what was said at Medellín and making concrete application to the situation in their respective countries. Unfortuntately, however, that is not the resolution of the matter. In Latin America it has always been normal to find an immense gap between verbal professions of position and the real-life fulfillment. And this is such a situation. Church leaders in Latin America have been traditionally allied with the oligarchs, the rich and the rulers. Only a small minority of them has effectively ended that alliance and dependence. Men like Camilo Torres and Che Guevara have died for justice, but there is still great need of men who will live and struggle for it, a task often more difficult than to die for an ideal. Small groups of priests in various countries have raised this banner, but justice needs many more defenders, and one can only hope that young men and women in increasing numbers will dedicate their lives to its cause.

I entertain no hope that the oligarchs will give up their lands and their ill-gotten wealth without violence. Neither do I believe that the present rulers, most of whom are themselves either members of the oligarchy or its stooges, will impose the rule of justice. The parallel between the condition of the poor in Latin America and that of the blacks in the United States is striking. Pressures and violence in the United States in recent years have brought a small measure of justice to the black community. And what is possibly more important, they have awakened the consciences of many white Americans who had previously been ignorant of the facts because they were not sufficiently interested to want to learn. I do not believe that the blacks in the United States will hold the small gains they have won unless they continue their pressure. The poor of Latin America must similarly create for themselves a power base and cause their voices to be heard. I am against all unnecessary violence, but I do not see how it can be avoided in many areas. In fact, the violence is already widely present, in the shape of repression of the poor by the rich and powerful. Because there is less democracy in Latin America than in the United States, fewer structures through which citizens can seek and demand social justice, I fear that more violence has to be anticipated here in the process of vindicating the rights of the poor.

The question I found it necessary to ask myself a long time ago, and which ultimately every priest has to ask himself, is where do I stand in relation to all of this. In the past, many priests were able to go through life living the role into which they were integrated and for which they were conditioned in the seminary. The priest had a very specific image of himself. He felt he was justifying his existence and fulfilling what was expected of him by carrying out the activities traditionally assigned to him: his ritual actions in celebrating Mass and conferring the sacraments, his supervision of pious societies, his social and bureaucratic functions.

Particularly since the Second Vatican Council, it has become increasingly difficult for priests to live with this kind of rationalization. They find it more difficult to justify the celebration of the Mass or the conferring of baptism or the other sacraments if the purpose of the recipient is simply to perform a social function, and even more when his intention is clearly superstitious. Yet many of us older priests, both those who are natives of the Latin American country in which they work and those who have come from outside, do not recognize the extent to which we have been brainwashed. We continue to see ourselves as fulfilling our total commitment by saving an abstraction which we call the soul rather than a living person composed of body and soul. We think we can fulfil this function by conferring the sacraments on people who have no understanding of the true spiritual significance of the actions we perform for them. We are content to exhort to virtue in circumstances which call for action to change structures that prevent man from being either virtuous or vicious because they maintain him in a subhuman condition. I know, because I have been part of that system. I remember once traveling for fourteen hours on horseback to the bedside of a man who was more than a hundred years old. When I reached him, my concern was to have him make his confession. He had never made a confession in his life. The only response I could get from him was that he wanted to feel a priest. He had been totally blind for years, but I moved close so that he could put his arm on my shoulder. In reply to my questions, he told me he had never committed any sins. He had not been married in the church. In fact, he had never been in a church in his life. He didn't know how many children he had, or how many wives. And for this I had ridden fourteen hours and killed the overwilling horse who carried me.

Camilo Torres formulated the problem of the priest in Latin America in terms I find particularly meaningful. In 1965 he said:

> My reasons for leaving the priesthood are the same ones that led me to embrace it. I discovered Christianity as a life completely centered on love for neighbor; I realized the value of being committed to this love . . . and so I chose the priesthood to become a servant of mankind. It was afterwards I found out that in Colombia you can't bring about this love just by beneficence, but that there was needed a change of political, economic and social structures, which demanded revolution. This love was intimately bound up with revolution. Unfortunately, in spite of the fact that my revolutionary activity found a broad response in the people, there came a moment when the ecclesiastical hierarchy wanted to silence me. That was against my conscience which led me to advocate revolution out of love for mankind. So to avoid all conflict with ecclesiastical discipline, I requested to be freed from being subject to its laws. Nevertheless, I consider myself a priest until eternity and I consider that my priesthood and its exercise is fulfilled in bringing about the Colombian revolution, in love for neighbor and in the struggle for the welfare of the majorities.

I suppose I can only say that I have been more fortunate than Camilo, in that I have never been forced to make a decision between my place as a priest within the Church institution and my understanding of my duty as a priest to bring Christ's good news to the poor and the oppressed. But more than once, as the story I have told in this book indicates, I thought myself very close to the dilemma. Fortunately for me, my ecclesiastical superiors showed themselves more understanding than those of Camilo Torres, and they respected my right to follow the road dictated to me by my conscience. I know that many of my fellow priests, more of them in the traditional past than in the updated present of the Church, questioned the utility or propriety of my work. Even if they recognized its objective validity, they could not see how it fitted into the priestly function as they conceived it.

To those of my fellow priests who honestly hold such views I can only appeal to reflect further on the reality of our involvement in causing and continuing the present unjust structures in Latin America. It seems to me impossible to claim that our only activity in the past was ''the saving of souls,'' when in fact we were a strong bulwark of the rich in their oppression of the poor. We preached resignation to the victims and we praised the generosity of the oppressor when he doled out scarcely enough to maintain the life of his workers. Today, the peasants in various countries are seizing land to feed their starving children, and in many cases, if not all, they are justified, according to the moral law, in taking this action. In these times is it not our right and duty to defend justice, to place ourselves in the front ranks of those seeking and doing justice?

But if Christians are to move into the front ranks of those seeking and doing justice, they have to realize who it is they are joining there. In the world as it is today, and in the world as its future outlines can be projected,

the people who have almost a monopoly on justice are
the disciples of Karl Marx. I think we have to be clear
about this. Celso Furtado, one of Brazil's major contemporary thinkers, once pointed out that every system has
a time in which it is right for human progress and development. At one time, feudalism was right as a way of life
calculated to move Europe forward. Then came the era
in which the factors coalesced to make capitalism viable
and carry mankind a significant step forward. But
capitalism's era of growth is over. It has worked for
some and may continue to work for them for a considerable time. But it is clear that it is not working and is
not going to work for the countries of Latin America
and the rest of the Third World of poverty. The system
that is now surging forward and upward is the one to
which Karl Marx gave its spirit and its thrust.

It is an astonishing coincidence that the two super-
prophets of the past two thousand years have both been
Jewish, Jesus Christ and Karl Marx. The total impact
of Christ on the development of humanity is at this time
far greater than that of Marx, because of the much longer
time his message has been inspiring and forming people.
But when it is remembered that it is only a century since
Marx wrote *Das Capital,* it has to be recognized that
the impact of Marx is proportionately far greater than
that of Christ during the first century after Marx. In
broad terms, the dominant influence on one-third of the
world's three billion inhabitants at the present time is
Christianity. Marxism similarly dominates the lives of
another third, and the remaining third is little affected
or influenced by either.

What fascinates me is to see how Christianity and
Marxism are steadily coming so much closer to each
other. In Christianity there has been a pluralism of
churches and ways of living the message of Christ almost
from the beginning, and now there is substantial pluralism

172   AGENT FOR CHANGE

even within each of the Christian churches, as the
Catholic Church in particular has been showing since
the Second Vatican Council. Marxism was long presented
to outsiders as an absolute monolith, and the first rulers
of Soviet Russia encouraged that image because it made
them the exclusive high priests of a world system. But
the pretense of a monolith has broken down hopelessly
under the impact of reality. We have a Russian style,
a Yugoslav style, a Chinese style, a Cuban style, etc.
We even have a Marx-inspired socialism of a non-
totalitarian kind in many European countries, of which
Sweden is probably the best example. Indeed, the Swedes
claim that their country has a far purer and more doc-
trinaire type of socialism than Soviet Russia. The essence
of socialism, they rightly say, is not state ownership of
the means of production, which is what characterizes
the state capitalism of the Soviet Union, but a control
of the means of production by the state to ensure that
they are utilized for the greatest good of the citizens,
which is the Swedish way. What I find most interesting
about this Swedish style is the major part the cooperative
movement plays in it. There one can see in actual practice
the contribution the cooperative movement can make in
a socialist state.

Leading Christian thinkers of Latin America have long
been openly stressing the need for a marriage of Christianity and Marxism. The influence of Marx can be clearly
seen in official pronouncements. I have already referred
to the analysis of the political, social, and economic situation of Latin America made by the bishops of the
hemisphere when they met in Medellín, Colombia, in
1968. Although they never mention Marx by name, their
language is straight out of his classical writings when
they denounce the oppressing power by which institutions
impose violence, the growing distortions of international
commerce, the neocolonialism of the national oligarchies

and the corresponding neocolonialism of the international monopolies, and the international imperialism of money. The reason the bishops did not want to give credit to Marx for their views was undoubtedly that they felt the many condemnations of Marxism by the popes made his teachings unacceptable. But in the future they will no longer have this restriction on their expression. In 1971, on the eightieth anniversary of Pope Leo XIII's historic encyclical on the social order, *Rerum novarum,* Pope Paul VI finally admitted that much truth was to be found in Marx. He openly affirmed the possibility of accepting "the elements of Marxist analysis" and of entering into "the practice of the class struggle."

This revised approach to Marx has been carried further by many Latin American theologians. In Bolivia, for example, Jordan Bishop says that far from denying or challenging the Christian vision of the world, that of Marxism complements it. Marxism, he says, is in a line of historical continuity with early Christianity, which was not only "communist" but also "materialist." The presence of a dynamic Christianity in a socialist society, Bishop asserts, can be "a presence as challenging as that of Camilo Torres in his feudal-capitalistic world." Archbishop Helder Camara of Recife, Brazil, is equally explicit when he says that he believes that we can have a socialism truly respectful of the human person.

In the same line of thought are such progressive Protestant theologians as Julio Barreiro, Joel Gajardo, and Rubem Alves. According to Barreiro, Marx never claimed that the communist society was the end of history, but only that communism was a real and necessary factor or step toward man's liberation. For Joel Gajardo, the greatest weakness of Christianity has been its failure to recognize that the class war is a fact, and that the privileged classes will continue to enjoy their privileges until the dispossessed acquire an awareness of their own strength. For Rubem Alves, the ultimate tragedy of the worker is not that he is poor, but that he is alienated and consequently unable to contribute to the building of a better society of the future.

I find myself very much at home with these schools of thought. As I see it, the Christianity which we preach and profess today retains perhaps 10 percent of the original message of Christ. It is a ship laden down with the barnacles of two thousand years, its legalism, its bureaucracy, its pride, its triumphalism, its lust for power and manipulation of the weak, all the phony things of which humans are capable. The fact is that man needs a combination of two virtues in order to be truly human, to be civilized, to be on a higher level than the other animals who at best can practice these virtues only partially and inadequately. These virtues are love or charity, and justice. For two thousand years the Catholic Church has placed the emphasis on charity, with little practical concern for justice. The Marxists stress justice, but they show little interest in love. But the fact is that neither of these virtues can flourish without the other without producing gross distortions. They need each other.

So what I look forward to is a marriage of the message of Christ with that of Karl Marx, a union of love and justice on which to build the new man of whom St. Paul spoke so eloquently. It may take centuries, though the speeding up of change in the modern time may shorten the period of preparation significantly. What I hope is that this union will take place without the enormous shedding of blood which accompanied the introduction of these two great prophets to the world, the martyrdoms of early Christian times and the religious wars which accompanied the later spread of Christianity and which are still with us today, the destruction of 25 million Russians in the making of the Soviet Union and who knows how many millions in the birth of communist China.

I have already indicated what I think Christianity will have to get rid of in order to make a true marriage with the justice of the Marxists, probably 90 percent of the distortions and irrelevancies which make it incredible to modern man. On the Marxist side, I think little change will be needed in the economic and social aspects. However, there are two major stumbling blocks, the ideological commitment to atheism, and the rigid controls over what people say and write. Fortunately, many Marxist thinkers are coming to recognize that the ideology which compels a denial of the existence of a personal God is not a scientific necessity. In this they agree with those Christian thinkers who say that we can accept Marxism as a pragmatic, empirically verifiable technique for social transformation without accepting the entire theoretic structure out of which this technique was originally derived. It is also clear that the harsh methods of thought control exercised in the initial period of the Soviet Union are being modified as the level of education and culture rises. Pressure for greater freedom of speech and publication is constantly growing, particularly among the young people who will soon be the decision makers.

Such, at least, is my vision of where we are going and my understanding of the theology of liberation which is being developed and spread by progressive Christians in Latin America. It forces us to see ourselves as involved historically in a process of freeing mankind from material and spiritual bondage, as assuming conscious responsibility for our own destiny. It is a call to all of us, especially to those who as priests and missionaries are potential agents for change, to work together for the creation of the new man and for the qualitatively different society in which he can achieve his full material and spiritual growth.